HOW TO BUILD A CULTURE

AN AUTHOR'S GUIDE TO BUILDING RICH AND DIVERSE CULTURES

A TREVENA

MAYTHORNE
PRESS

ISBN: 9781838327378

Cover art by P&V Digital

Published by Maythorne Press
www.maythornepress.co.uk

How to Build a Culture is also available as an ebook Guidebook.

The content of the ebook is the same. It offers a more portable version of this workbook, and simply requires you to provide your own space for notes.

AUTHOR GUIDES SERIES

30 DAYS OF WORLDBUILDING SECOND EDITION
An Author's Step-by-Step Guide to Building Fictional Worlds

HOW TO DESTROY THE WORLD
An Author's Guide to Writing Dystopia and Post-Apocalypse

FROM SANCTITY TO SORCERY
An Author's Guide to Building Belief Structures and Magic Systems

HOW TO CREATE HISTORY
An Author's Guide to Creating History, Myths, and Monsters

HOW TO BUILD A CULTURE
An Author's Guide to Building Rich and Diverse Cultures

stepbystepworldbuilding.com

CONTENTS

INTRODUCTION

I am one of those authors who have been writing, pretty much, since they were old enough to hold a pen. I have a folder of old stories, typed up on an old typewriter, that I don't even remember having written.

I was rarely seen without a book in my hand, and spent every spare hour I had, buried deep in fantastical worlds. I was lucky that my parents encouraged it. They never told me that I was wasting my time, or to keep my head out of the clouds. They even let me read at the dinner table, eating one-handed.

I was also lucky to have access to a local library, and quickly worked my way through the fantasy catalogue in their children's section. I swept my way through all of the Choose Your Own Adventure books; not only following the adventures of kids—passing into a fantasy world to fight dragons, mounted on their bicycle steeds—but I got to control the stories. I could re-read them over and over, choosing different paths each time, creating a multitude of adventures for myself.

My love of speculative fiction had started young. It was my dad's job to read the bedtime stories each night, all of us huddled together to listen. He often picked books from his own collection which, almost exclusively, consisted of classic sci-fi novels. And so, as a child, my bedtime stories were written by the likes of H.G. Wells and John Wyndham. Looking back, I suspect that *The War of the Worlds* and *The Day of the Triffids* were probably inappropriate choices for children about to go to sleep, but it must have caught my imagination. I will forever thank my dad for introducing me to such tales.

At the age of 16 I finally picked up the Chronicles of Narnia books, reading all seven of them in just five days. It was then that my Narnia obsession began, and it has never waned.

Before starting at university, I worked in an antique auction house. Every wardrobe that came through the saleroom, I would check in the back of it for Narnia. It reached the point where my colleagues would come and inform me each time they took receipt of one!

When they announced the latest film adaptations, I scoured the internet daily for news. I saw each of them on their day of release, going to the cinema alone for an uninterrupted experience. A pure absorption of them. I can still name the four actors who portrayed the Pevensie children, their names branded into my memory. Yes, the woman who can't even remember her own phone number!

One of my most treasured possessions is an old wardrobe. I bought it from a second-hand furniture shop for just £20. It has moved house with us several times, and has practically fallen apart, with my husband tasked with fixing it back together. Carved into its door is a beautiful rendering of a ship, in full sail, riding the sea. And the serpentine hinges on it are like sea monsters. It is beautiful, and largely useless. It isn't deep enough to hold a standard coat hanger on its rail, and the mirror on the back of the door is so mottled and degraded it hardly reflects anything at all. In fact, it has rarely ever been used as an actual wardrobe, and currently holds my increasingly out of control to-be-read pile.

But, because it looks like it may have once stood in the captain's quarters on board the Dawntreader, I will never part with it.

And, over the years, I have collected other bits and pieces that remind me of Narnia. Including film props, and a good collection of behind-the-scenes and the-making-of books. My obsession is complete, and incurable. All that is left is to find a way to Narnia myself. I'm still looking, and I won't give up.

Despite this, I did stray from my love of fantasy. At university I studied Drama and Creative Writing, and wandered away from magic and fantastical worlds. I can't say why, it just happened. Perhaps I felt pressure to finally grow up. Perhaps my university course pushed me towards literary fiction. Perhaps I simply needed a break from it for a while. I don't know.

After university, as I began to navigate the confusing and cynical world of adulthood, I barely read anything at all. For a long time, I hardly managed a handful of books a year. During this time, I read my first ever Stephen King book. It was, interestingly enough, *On Writing* that I picked up first, and I finished it in just a few days. And so, I was brought back to literature with a renewed desire to read, as well as to write.

Although I've been writing since I was very young, it was never my ambition to make a career from it. I wanted to act. I wanted to be on stage. My whole childhood was filled with drama lessons, singing lessons, lessons in several different forms of dance. I was always performing: music concerts, amateur dramatics, school plays. If there was a spotlight, I was in it.

While I was at university, studying Drama, I discovered that I wasn't enjoying it as much as I'd expected to. I had a long heart-to-heart with myself, finally accepting that the ambition I'd had all of my life, my singular goal, simply wasn't what I wanted anymore. And it was difficult to let go of. This vision had shaped my entire life, my entire personality, and I had nothing to replace it with.

But I couldn't pretend to myself anymore. And, as I continued with my degree, I came to the conclusion that I didn't want to be onstage, blinking into the spotlight, speaking someone else's words. What I wanted was to sit in the back of a darkened auditorium, watching other people perform my words. I wanted to write.

Even with this revelation, I still didn't imagine myself making writing into any kind of a career. The first Kindle wouldn't come on the market for another six years. The publishing landscape was a very different one to what it is today. Becoming a published author was a pipe-dream. One that seemed to rely far more on luck than any kind of talent. A who-you-know rather than a what-you-know industry. And for a young woman barely into her twenties, and still reeling from losing the footing of the one constant she'd had in her life, it all seemed like an impossibility.

As part of my Creative Writing class, our tutor asked us to write a personal introduction to an imaginary book about ourselves. Much like this introduction you're reading right now. The difference being, in that hypothetical introduction, I wrote "I can't imagine writing ever being anything more than a hobby for me." When I wrote that, I wouldn't have believed I'd ever be writing one for real.

When our assignments were returned, my tutor had highlighted that sentence, responding with the note "Based on your writing, that would be a shame." That single comment began a shift in mindset which, over the following years, led me to this moment right now. And this book, through all those that have come before it.

Inspiration tends to come from the most unexpected sources, at the most unexpected of moments.

And I'm sure that my tutor has no idea of the impact she had. Of the wheels she set into motion. Of the future she helped to craft. She dropped a small pebble into a pool, and its ripples are still radiating outwards.

USING THIS WORKBOOK

If you'd like to deepen and expand a world you've created, this is the book for you. If your characters are set to encounter an unfamiliar culture, and you want to make it distinct and separate from their own, this is the book for you. If you're looking to build your first fictional society, and you're not sure where to start, this is definitely the book for you.

This workbook is broken into easy, manageable prompts for you to complete. If you work your way through, even if you only complete one prompt per day, in just over a month, you will have created a rich and diverse culture for your characters to exist in.

This list of prompts is not, by any means, exhaustive. Depending on your genre, your story, your characters, and the world you need to create for them, you may need aspects that are not covered by this workbook. Likewise, some of these prompts may not be relevant to you.

Think of it like a garden. This book gives you the foundation to build upon. It helps you to plant the seeds, and offers you seeds you may not have considered planting yourself. But you'll need to cultivate it, and water it. And you may have plants of your own that you want to include. A special tree, your favourite flower. You may like to have a pond, or a bench, or a marquee.

The other thing this workbook offers is a safe, singular place to keep all of your worldbuilding notes. It's surprisingly easy to get lost in your own world, and surprisingly easy to forget the details of it. This will become your worldbuilding bible. Your one-stop-shop for everything you need to know about your world's culture. When you come to writing your story, keep this book next to you, so that everything you need to know is in easy reach.

This workbook is packed with direct questions to answer and tables to fill in, as well as a space at the back for all of those ideas that don't quite belong. Not yet, at least.

Above all, enjoy your worldbuilding. Enjoy exploring it, and watching it come to life around you.

As a simple human, this may be the closest you'll come to performing real magic. To visualise an entire world from nothing. To pluck things from the air and make them real. To take breath on the wind and form it into something tangible. That is the most real, purest magic I know of.

Of course, I'm being presumptuous here. You may have magical abilities beyond my comprehension. In fact, you may even be a little more than human...

WORLDBUILDING BASICS

While fantasy and science-fiction authors may be doing the heavy lifting when creating their fictional worlds, worldbuilding exists in, pretty much, every genre. To a certain extent.

Whether it's the creation of an imaginary cafe in a real town, or imagining an alternative outcome to an event from history, any book, of any kind, can involve worldbuilding. At the fantasy, sci-fi, and horror end of the scale, the worldbuilding-heavyweights, it may mean the creation of a magic system, or monsters, to slot alongside the real world. Or it may mean building an entirely new world with new species and cultures, right up to an entire universe of planets.

It can become quite the epic task!

Now, I don't know about you, but I tend to get easily overwhelmed by epic tasks. That's why I'm still working up to de-cluttering my house. I just look at the job as a whole, can't untangle where to actually start, and I end up doing nothing at all.

As much as I understand the usefulness and the importance of breaking things down into workable chunks, into simple steps, the ability and method for doing this very often escapes me. Unlike many other people, I can see the wood very clearly. It's the trees I have trouble with.

And this is what this workbook is designed to do. It breaks the task of building a fully fictional world into sizeable chunks. 30 of them. If you simply complete one task per day, by the end of the month, you will have a whole world to begin writing in, or to continue building into finer detail.

One task a day. That's not difficult or scary, is it?

Worldbuilding doesn't need to be difficult, or complicated. It doesn't need to take forever, or be an excuse for never actually writing the book. It doesn't need to be overwhelming or intimidating. At the other end of the scale, it shouldn't be something that you haphazardly bolt on in a last-minute panic.

As you'll discover through this book, worldbuilding should be tightly integrated with your plot and your characters. Your characters, and their goals, their struggles, their journey, are the reason your readers show up. That's the reason they keep reading. You can have the most amazing world, but if you don't populate it with compelling, sympathetic, and relatable characters, readers will simply stop turning the pages. Likewise, if you write amazing characters, and put them into a flat, paper world, your readers won't want to walk along with them, or explore with them.

Just as you want your readers to believe in your characters, you want them to believe in your world, too.

Let them smell the salt on the breeze, hear the buzzing of the insects. Let them feel the heat of the burning buildings, and feel the oppression of the government. Let them walk every single step with your characters. Invite them in. And invite them to stay. Whether they want to set up home there, or fight to change it.

Your worldbuilding is equally as important as your story and characters. Give your characters somewhere real to live, and give your readers somewhere real to visit. You simply can't separate these things out if you want to write the best book that you can.

So, what are you waiting for? Let's get started with the basics of worldbuilding.

DIFFERENT TYPES OF WORLDBUILDING

There are a few different ways to approach worldbuilding, and which you choose, will depend on your goals, your story, and your genre.

Building a whole new fictional world:
This is mostly used for writing fantasy and science fiction, and involves creating an entirely fictional world from scratch. Somewhere that does not, and never has, existed. It may have similarities to our world, and it may have huge differences. Think along the lines of second-world fantasies penned by the likes of J.R.R. Tolkien or C.S. Lewis.

A real place with an alternative past or future:
This may be taking a real existing place, London, for example, and giving it an alternative or altered history. Imagine if the Great Fire of London had actually been started by dragons. How would that change the world today? Or it may be taking the real-world place, and throwing it into your imagined future. This is very common in dystopia, imagining an unpleasant future for our world.

When using this style of worldbuilding, your map is usually, largely, already done for you. There is likely to be some changes, such as missing landmarks, or different names for places. The extent of the changes would entirely depend on your story, and how different you have imagined the past or future of this place.

A real place with a parallel fictional world:
The other way is to set your story in a real place, and have a fictional world created alongside it, usually invisible or hidden from the general public. Such as in Neil Gaiman's Neverwhere, or Harry Potter, or Hellboy. The fictional side of the world may be tightly integrated with the real world, or it may be quite separate. This would depend, again, on your story.

Whichever kind of world you're building, your objective is still the same: to create a believable world that your readers can really imagine walking around in.

MAP MAKING

One of my favourite parts of worldbuilding is making the map. You don't need to be an amazing artist; a child-like scrawl on the back of an envelope is good enough, as long as it makes sense to you and prevents you from getting lost in your own world. Which, believe me, is surprisingly easy.

Imagine your characters are travelling from A to B. If, in one chapter, B lies west of A and then, suddenly, it's south, your readers will notice. Or if B is a coastal town one minute, and a village in the mountains the next, your readers will notice, and it will drag them out of your story. Plus, they will love to call you up on it. They'll email you. They'll message you on social media. And they'll write it in their reviews.

As an author, your job is to keep them in the story. To keep them believing in it. To blur out their real world, their real life, and construct a new one for them, for as long as they're reading your book. Glaring inaccuracies will pluck them out of your world. Inaccuracies break the illusion, and remind them that they are simply reading a story. That they're not a hero fighting against a terrible foe. It pulls them back to their own cold, harsh, boring reality. And no one wants that!

And so, at the writing stage, your world map is for you. If you're not confident in your artistic abilities, there are plenty of artists who can create a stunning map to go into the front of your book. At this stage, the map is only for your eyes. Build it out of Lego, build it on Minecraft, mould it from clay, or cake, or whatever. As long as it's useful to you (and you're not tempted to eat it!)

And don't be tempted to simply draw a map and then randomly scatter towns across it. That doesn't happen, it's not believable. Towns are founded in specific places for specific reasons. The main reason being, of course, survival.

So, imagine you're choosing a place to establish a town. What do you need? What considerations do you need to make?

Fresh water source:
The most important and first consideration. Have you ever noticed how many major cities have a river flowing through them?

Varied food source:
Man cannot live by bread alone. Or cake, sadly. Their food source needs to be varied enough to keep them healthy.

Natural resources:
They need enough resources to be able to build their homes, and the things they need. They can also use these resources for trade.

Appropriate land for crops/animals:
The landscape they choose to settle in will hugely impact the kind of food and animals they farm.

Access and security:
Can they get in and out of their settlement easily while still keeping it protected from intruders?

Trade route:
Can traders visit their settlement? Is it on a major trade route, or will they have to rely on people making a special trip?

Predators:
What lives in the woods? Or the mountains? How do they protect themselves against it?

People, by and large, will choose the easiest option for their home, unless the benefits outweigh the dangers or struggles. For example, you might consider it foolish to establish a town in the middle of a dragon breeding ground. But what if just one dragon scale (which could be naturally shed) would sell for a price that could feed a family for three months. Then, it may well be worth it.

NAMING PLACES

There are several different ways to name the places on your map. Remember that it's not just towns and cities you need to name. Depending on how big your map is, you might be naming mountain ranges, rivers, forests, counties, countries, oceans, continents, or even planets.

Just like places on your map aren't randomly placed, neither are they randomly named. They might be named after their founder, or the landscape, or the natural resources, the wildlife, the river or mountain they're close to. They might be named after a local legend; your place names can actually conjure up stories of their own.

Of course, you can backward engineer these things. You can find the name for a place, and then create the reason it was named that. Perhaps no one remembers. Perhaps it doesn't matter to you, or your characters, or your story. As I'll discuss in the next section, you don't need a full and complete history for everything.

There are so many online naming generators. Simply do a search, and you'll find countless. I have two that I favour:

- squid.org/rpg-random-generator
- seventhsanctum.com

HISTORY

Your current world is a product of everything that ever happened there, even if no one in your world still remembers. It's your job, as the writer, to know. To remember what they can't.

I'm not saying that you need to plot out 5 million years' worth of history. Unless you're into that. Some people are. But you definitely need to know enough to understand why things are the way they are. To know enough to effectively create the world, its culture, and values.

As people, we act according to our culture. And each culture is different. And there are variations in that culture. The things we value. The things we see as rude, or polite, or unnecessary. The things we want, the things we avoid. Religion. Festivals. The way we treat our elderly. The way we treat children. The kind of food we eat, and the way in which we eat it. The kind of jobs we do. The differences between rich and poor. The differences between high culture and low culture.

And these things change over time. Invading cultures. Migrating cultures. Important events. A war, or a natural disaster can hugely change a place's culture. Changing what's important to them. Changing the way they live their lives.

And you need to remember that every time something changes, it affects everything else.

There are different levels at which an event can occur.

International events:
Something that affects the entire world. Like climate change, population explosion, the sun dying, zombie apocalypse, etc

National events:
Something that affects the country or large area. Like an economic crash, natural disasters, death of a monarch, etc.

Local events:
Something that affects a town or community. Harvest failure, flood, local elections, introduction of a new predator, a new trade deal, etc.

Individual events:
Something that affects one person or family. Bereavement, loss of employment, loss of home, births, marriages, a lottery win, etc.

It's obvious how an international event affects everything else. I'm sure a worldwide zombie outbreak would affect you and your family. But what about the other way round?

So, imagine a family preparing for a wedding. They order a whole load of wine from the next village. That gives the farmer enough money to finally live out his dream of buying a boat and exploring the seas. When the winter rains come, the lack of the vineyard on the hillside causes a landslip which demolishes the mining town below, which leads to a shortage of minerals, which leads to a shortage of coins, which results in an economic crash.

This is, of course, a somewhat extreme example, but it's an important thing to bear in mind. Think about the butterfly effect, and the ripples you might be sending out.

Imagine your world as a pool. Every event, ever construct, every thing you change or create, is like dropping a pebble into the water. Sometimes, the ripples last a few minutes. Sometimes, a few years. Spreading wider. Affecting more people. Sometimes, those ripples last for centuries.

HOW YOUR WORLD AFFECTS CHARACTER AND STORY

You can also use your worldbuilding to create conflict. Remember that conflict is created when your protagonist's goal is interrupted, or opposed, and you can use your world to do that.

Perhaps the most obvious example is if the protagonist's goal requires them to break the law. But you can use other things too: limitations of magic, social norms and expectations, gender roles. The landscape itself can become a physical barrier, or the weather, or a lack of resources.

And you can use all of this in your worldbuilding to raise the stakes. To increase the tension.

Because your world doesn't exist separately from the people who live in it, and you should create it with those people in mind. They will have opinions about everything. Beliefs, hopes, grievances. Things they love, things they hate. Things they want to change. Things they fight to change.

And these things will differ based on all of their nuances: gender, age, class, religion, etc. So their opinions will be different to the person stood next to them. They may even directly oppose one another. Conflict.

You have to remember that everything comes back to character. You have to remember that you aren't writing a story about a world that happens to have people living in it. You are writing a story about people who happen to live in a particular world.

Worldbuilding. Story. Character. None of these is independent from the others.

A NOTE ABOUT CULTURE

When you're creating your culture, always bear in mind that it is a fluid thing. It changes and shifts over time. But it is also stubborn and it's rooted deep. From the moment someone is born, their culture is imprinted upon them. From their parents, from their peers, from every interaction. When they step beyond the norms, they are tugged back through correction, reproach, punishment. Urged back onto the path.

But with every new generation, every new age, culture shifts. It might happen incrementally, steadily, step by step. Or it might happen suddenly. Something might force the culture to shift. Something might force a shrugging off of the old ways, the old ideas.

It might be an uprising, a revolution. It might be the people saying "enough is enough", or "this isn't fair". It might be a welcome change, or it might be fiercely contested. Or the change might come from above. A new monarch, a new authority, bringing in a new outlook. It might be the leadership of a country changing from secular to religious, or civilian to military. The changes might be gently fed in, allowing people to adjust. It might be enforced through firepower.

Culture changes as people migrate and move around the world. It changes when science, medicine, or technology advances. As new knowledge and understanding is enveloped. It changes when wars happen, natural disasters, economic crashes. Sometimes it changes for the better, sometimes for the worse. Depending on your perspective.

Humans like to define things. They like to understand the world. While their understanding of the world is influenced, heavily, by the cultural lens they look through, it is their desire to make sense of things, to neatly categorise and label things, that informs their culture. It's cyclical. One thing feeding from the other, around and around.

Understanding things is safety. If people understand what is good for them, and what harms them, they stay alive. They stay healthy. Humans like things that make sense. They like the familiar. They enjoy routine and predictability and stability. And when the ground begins to shift, people instinctually grasp hold of something strong and unmoving. They reach for something they can rely on. Be it their mother's hand, a weapon, or a cultural norm.

When change happens, people push back. Because they're being asked to shrug off the familiar to adopt the new and unfamiliar. It's hard, and difficult, and scary. People resist. They resist with anger, they resist with refusal, they resist with rebellion. Even when it doesn't affect them directly. Even when it improves things. It doesn't matter. When the ground moves beneath them, it feels just as shaky, either way.

With this in mind, let's build a culture...

THE ARTS

The arts is probably the most obvious place to begin. When we think about the term 'culture', we often think about art galleries, theatres, sculptures. We might think about great, epic poems, and songs, and legends passed down the generations through storytelling.

There is so much more to culture than this, and the arts are just one little part of it. But they are a very reflective part. The arts hold up a mirror to the culture of a society, and they reflect everything they see: the beauty as well as the flaws. It is a space in which we can explore and examine culture, a way in which artists can highlight, subvert, and caricature culture, leading us to focus in on one aspect or another.

Importantly, through the arts, we're able to see our culture in new ways, with new eyes, new perspectives and angles. We can see it from a view we've never had before. We can see it as someone else sees it, rather than simply accepting it as it is. And by seeing it anew, we can begin to question it, and even to challenge it.

Throughout history, across the whole of our world, art has been controversial. It has been confronting and divisive. It has been dangerous. It has challenged and upset the status quo. It has pushed at the pedestal of power, tipped it, and attempted to topple it. And so, art has been banned. Artists have been silenced. Sometimes, permanently.

Being an artist hasn't always been safe. It isn't safe everywhere in the world now. Which, arguably, may make it all the more important.

So, when you're thinking about the place art has in your world, don't just think about ladies and gentlemen sedately browsing a gallery. Don't just think about them dressing up to attend the theatre. The theatre was once a rowdy place, full of noise and fighting, prostitutes, traders, heckling. It wasn't always the dignified experience it has become.

Art can be loud. It can be unpalatable. It can even take up arms.

When you're thinking about the arts in your own world, remember to also think about the artists themselves. From the famous musicians and renowned sculptors down to the people embroidering beautiful designs in their village and those performing traditional dances each harvest festival.

Art can be personal and private. It can have a small, local audience. It can be mass-produced, replicated in plastic and shipped across the world. It can be unique one-off pieces that dominate the horizon and last for centuries. Equally, it can be a drawing rendered in sand and left to be erased by the encroaching tide.

Perhaps your culture is one that celebrates art, that idolises those producing it. Maybe creativity is valued deeply, perhaps more than anything else, encouraged and fostered in every child and adult. Maybe your world's health system is based on art therapies, with doctors prescribing a dance class or a lace-making course instead of ointments and creams. Perhaps your magic system is based in music, or jewellery making. Perhaps spells are woven into rugs or stitched into garments.

The government's budget for arts funding may greatly outstrip its defence budget. Perhaps there are more galleries in your society than there are coffee shops. Maybe every single wall, every inch of plain space, is decorated with artwork. The air filled with the sound of music, the streets designed for dancing, not driving.

It may make for a peaceful, harmonious society. Or the constant sensory overload may have created widespread mental health issues, with people purposefully damaging their sight and hearing to escape from it.

On the flip side, you may create a culture that vilifies art, that outlaws it. Maybe it's widely viewed as shameful, something only ever whispered about, or practised in secret. There may be certain arts that are allowed, while others are banned. There may be subject matter that no one will explore, with harsh punishments for those who do.

The arts may have been commandeered by the government, used to push propaganda, to tell legends filled with patriotic themes, to instil obedience and compliance. Artists might require licences to display their work, may only be able to display or share it in registered properties, need to sign a code of conduct, or have their work inspected before making it public.

Artists may be viewed as outsiders, as breaking societal norms. They might be viewed as radicals, as anarchists or troublemakers. Perhaps they're thought of as spiritually elevated, as shamans with a connection to other worlds. Maybe it's thought that they are directly inspired by God, or have a way of glimpsing heaven.

Artists may be viewed as childlike, as dreamers who never grew up. They might be seen as wasting their time, as people who failed to fit into society properly. They might be a vital part of society, the only ones able to write, or honoured with the responsibility of chronicling history.

In later prompts, we'll be looking at the accessibility of art, at which art forms are widely available, and which are more elite. For now, I'd like you to consider the overall view of art that your culture holds, the kinds of arts that are practised, and how artists are perceived.

This will be heavily influenced by how liberal and free your culture is. Laws, restrictions, and regulations will sway people towards mistrust of the arts. Either as self-preservation, or indoctrination. Widely available and celebrated art will raise up the attitudes towards artists. The way historical artworks are valued and preserved, from paintings and photographs, to buildings and monuments, will impact how modern art is viewed. Is it a legacy for the future, or a valueless snippet to be discarded and forgotten?

DIFFERENT TYPES OF ART IN YOUR WORLD:
THE GENERAL ATTITUDE TOWARDS THE ARTS:

THE ROLE THE ARTS PLAY IN:

RECORDING HISTORY:
REFLECTING/SATIRISING SOCIETY:
CHALLENGING THE STATUS QUO:
EDUCATION:
LEISURE TIME:
EVERYDAY LIFE:

HOW THE ARTS ARE FUNDED:
HOW ARTISTS ARE TREATED:
HOW CONTROVERSIAL ART IS TREATED:
RESTRICTIONS ON THE ARTS:
LAWS REGARDING THE ARTS:
HOW ACCESSIBLE ARE THE ARTS?

POPULAR CULTURE

When thinking about popular culture, I want you to consider the forms of art that are widely available, easily accessed, and consumed on a large scale. Sometimes called 'low culture', it is mass-produced, beamed into every home, readily available, and generally cheap and disposable.

Think about libraries, television, popular music. Think about the arts that are readily available, constantly to hand, that sit on the 'top 10' and 'new and popular' shelves in shops. Think about the arts that are talked about widely, the songs sung in pubs, the movies streamed on demand.

It's difficult to think about popular culture without comparing it to 'high culture', which trips you into a pattern of viewing popular culture as 'lowly' and 'less than', and aimed at the 'less educated'. It suggests that popular culture is 'unchallenging' and not designed to 'make you think'. Don't dismiss this as simply incidental.

Making this 'better' and 'worse' distinction in the arts, maintains the 'us' and 'them' distinction between different demographics of society. By creating an attitude of elitism around 'high culture', those engaging in it can feel superior. Remember that, very often, wealthy patrons have visited places such as the opera and ballet in order to be seen there. They have settled themselves into their private boxes in full view of the cheaper seats below. At the Elizabethan theatre, those who could spare the money could afford a cushion to sit on, while the 'groundlings' simply stood in the 'pit' or 'yard'. While all levels of society attended the theatre, they were segregated, and easily differentiated.

You may be creating a fully egalitarian society, in which case, you will have to think carefully about how to make the arts fully accessible on an entirely level pegging. Look at the segregation and elitism that exists in your own culture, and then consider how to make it equal in your fictional world. How to remove the distinctions. Think about the ways that art belongs to everyone in your world, both in regards to consuming it and creating it.

But you can also use the distinction between popular and high culture to highlight segregation in your world and create conflict in your story. Remember: it may not be a segregation based on wealth and socio-economics.

Beyond money, there are many other barriers that may stop people from accessing the arts, or particular parts of it. Location, disability, language, religion, amount of leisure time, childcare. These are all potential barriers to accessing the arts. Perhaps there are rules and regulations that prevent certain people from accessing certain arts based on their gender, ethnicity, or magical ability.

And when you're thinking about who can access the arts as a consumer, as a viewer, also consider who can *practice* these disciplines. Perhaps music is only taught in certain schools, or theatre is only practised by girls, or only magicians are allowed to paint. On the flip side, consider how the arts might be made accessible to people who are deaf, blind, or physically disabled.

And don't fall into the trap of thinking that the popular culture of your world shouldn't be challenging. That it shouldn't raise questions or encourage deep-thinking. While the arts can be used as pure escapism and simple enjoyment—a way to relax and unwind after a busy day—it can also be thought-provoking, satirical, or multi-layered with deeper subtext. Just because it's widely available, doesn't mean it has to be 'dumbed down'.

The ways in which popular culture is accessed in your world will depend on many things. Technology being a big one. Mass-produced and print-on-demand books, or artwork. Televisions in homes. The Internet, first at home, and then in our pockets, on the move. Technology has hugely transformed how we consume popular culture. I can stream movies on the train. I can download images of famous artworks as desktop wallpaper. I can go on a virtual tour of a museum, or see the seven wonders of the world via satellite imagery.

The closer to home that art can be accessed, the more widely consumed it can become. The less effort someone needs to put in to consume it, the more likely they are to do so. If art requires travel, an entrance fee, childcare, a new dress, a pair of smart shoes; each of those things are a hurdle. And sometimes, too much of a barrier.

Does this kind of easy access diminish the value of art? That's a question you'll have to answer for the culture you're creating.

And your world might not have this kind of easy access. Perhaps few people can even read, let alone write. Maybe paper is expensive. Maybe people don't have access to art materials. Perhaps they don't have leisure time outside of their working hours.

But this is where folk art can thrive. While the cities have their theatres and galleries, smaller communities will be adding embellishments to their clothing, decorating their homes, and creating beautiful things in their own ways. Folk art might become popular. It might become sought-after. It might be appropriated from those who created it, and churned out in factories. Printed on coffee cups, pasted onto t-shirts, formed in plastic. Removed from the subculture that created it. Losing its meaning. Or rural communities might grow wealthy by selling original, traditional crafts, pushing up the price of authentic pieces. Popularity of a subculture can also save it. Protect it.

Popular culture can take the arts in many different directions. Don't think that it only cheapens things. Don't think that it just makes art disposable and trivialised. Popular culture allows people to access art who wouldn't have before, either by choice or circumstance. It can bring culture, inspiration, and entertainment to everyone, no matter their situation. It can encourage creativity, and spark ambition. It can teach empathy, offer new experiences, and increase understanding of the world. It can bring the unreachable into easy reach.

WHICH OF THE ARTS ARE ACCESSIBLE AS POPULAR CULTURE?
HOW IS POPULAR CULTURE ACCESSED?
HOW HAS CHANGING TECHNOLOGY IMPACTED POPULAR CULTURE?
HOW HAS POPULAR CULTURE IMPACTED TRADITIONAL ARTS AND CRAFTS?
HOW HAS POPULAR CULTURE IMPACTED ATTITUDES TOWARDS THE ARTS?

HIGH CULTURE

While popular culture is easily accessible and produced en masse, high culture is the other side of the coin. It is usually elitist, exclusive, and inaccessible to many.

High culture includes the arts that are considered 'better', 'posher', or 'more civilised'. They might be thought of as being more intellectually stimulating or more advanced, requiring a higher level of skill or training than the arts included in popular culture. Performers and artists are likely to be more revered and idolised, considered to be more talented than their popular peers.

People might believe that dislike of high culture is due to a misunderstanding of it. That those unable to appreciate it lack the civility or intelligence to enjoy it. Likes and dislikes in popular culture are mostly seen as subjective, while dislikes of high culture are sometimes considered to be a failing on the part of the viewer.

If you are creating an egalitarian society, with equal access to the arts for everyone, it might be more difficult to have any kind of distinction between high culture and popular culture. Once high culture is opened to the masses, and accessible to everyone, then, by definition, surely it becomes popular culture. And if you separate out high culture by means of limitation (limited number of shows, limited number of editions printed, etc), then you will need to think carefully about how you avoid creating inequality. If the limited nature of something pushes up its value, you lose your level playing field. If certain cultural events are limited to certain locations or times of year, you're putting up barriers for those who can't travel, or those who work at certain times. You may have arts that are better thought of, that require more training, but the access to them would need to be the same as any other.

But, let's look how how high culture can be used in a less equal society. It can be used to cause division, to encourage snobbery, and to perpetuate a view of 'us' and 'them'.

And bear in mind, that you're not simply creating inequality for inequality's sake. Even if you're writing a dystopian story, or a cyberpunk story, or writing a story to purposefully highlight inequality, prejudice, and oppression, it still needs to have a direct impact and function in your story and the journeys of your characters. Always ask yourself: is it pushing the plot forwards? Is it revealing character? It can, absolutely, be used to reveal worldbuilding and themes in your story, but it's all the better if it has a direct, active impact too.

What happens when a low-class character attends the opera? What happens when someone from a disadvantaged background dreams of performing ballet? What happens when a musical prodigy is discovered in the slums?

But the distinctions don't need to be solely economic. Maybe only men can attend the theatre. Perhaps only those with white skin can enter art galleries. It might be that music can only be performed by those with magical powers. Or that a qualification from a single university is required if you wish to publish your writing. The history of our world is filled with examples of exclusivity in the arts: certain people excluded from universities, or performing on stages, or publishing under their real name. While you can choose to reflect and highlight real-world incidences, you also have the freedom to be more creative. Or to focus on a different form of inequality, or make a different social comment. Or to simply have fun pushing your characters around.

But the differentiation between high and popular culture, and the exclusivity of the latter, offer numerous opportunities to create conflict in the culture you create. You can say a lot about your world by the kinds of artistic pursuits that sit in each category. You don't need to include ballet, opera, and classical music in high culture. Perhaps ballet is performed in dingy pubs and bars. Maybe opera is sung in school playgrounds. Likewise, you can subvert what constitutes popular culture in your world. Maybe your society views older forms of art out-of-date and disposable. Maybe it's the newly created art that fetches the highest price.

Think about the world you're creating, and think about what your society might value, and why. What would they consider to be more worthy of their time and patronage? Is age a determining factor? Perhaps historical importance or, maybe, arts that are pro-government are pushed into the 'high culture' category, while arts that criticise and satirise the government are written off as 'low culture', and unworthy of status or respect.

Does high culture have the freedom to criticise the status quo? Or does it seek to uphold it? Consider what might happen to a high culture artist who decided to be more controversial. And think about who benefits from the exclusivity of high culture. Who's kept out of it, and why?

Consider how the values of your society may have changed over time. Think about which high culture artists might fall out of favour, and why. Cancel culture isn't just a feature of modern society, there are many examples of it throughout history. In fact, ostracisation by popular vote was used as a punishment thousands of years ago. And there was a time that expulsion from your tribe almost certainly led to your death, unable to survive outside and alone.

WHICH OF THE ARTS ARE CONSIDERED TO BE HIGH CULTURE?

HOW IS ACCESS TO HIGH CULTURE RESTRICTED?
WHO IS UNABLE, OR LESS ABLE, TO ACCESS HIGH CULTURE?
WHAT ARE THE ATTITUDES TOWARDS HIGH CULTURE ARTISTS, AND HOW DO THEY DIFFER TO POPULAR ARTISTS?
HOW HAS HIGH CULTURE CHANGED OVER TIME?
WHAT SUBJECT MATTERS DOES HIGH CULTURE AVOID, AND HOW IS THAT GOVERNED?

COMMUNICATION AND THE SPREAD OF IDEAS

You may be writing a world in which news, gossip, and information travels only by word-of-mouth, carried by passing traders, travelling minstrels, and pilgriming monks. Maybe communication is by way of written letters, carried across the country by wagon, mail coach, or steam train. Perhaps the telephone exists, or email, or long-distance telepathy.

For this particular prompt, we're looking at personal communication: gossip, stories, anecdotes, and opinions. We'll look at the more formalised spread of official news and information in a later prompt. So, consider the kind of ideas that might be spread by informal means. Much of it might be false, misunderstood, misinterpreted. It may be second, or third hand information. It might be based on someone's personal opinion or prejudice. It may not be very reliable at all.

What methods do people have to fact check? To investigate or research further? Is it a simple task online, or are they left to either dismiss or accept the information on gut feeling? Remember that people are more likely to believe something if it aligns with their own personal experience or viewpoint. And it's easy to dismiss something you disagree with.

But this spread of informal communication can have a big impact on the culture of your world, and the things that people believe about the society they live in.

Think about the main forms of communication in your world. How likely is it that the original message might be misheard, tampered with, or misinterpreted?

We all know that a story told orally over and over is often changed. The heroes might become more heroic, the villains more villainous, and the battle between them far more bloody. People forget details, add in their own, or forget the ending entirely. A message can become something wildly different by the time it finds the intended recipient. Letters can be intercepted and changed, having extra paragraphs and postscripts added into empty space, or be re-written altogether. Telephone calls suffer from a lack of body language (Albert Mehrabian, a researcher of body language, concluded that 55% of communication is nonverbal). Text messages and social media posts can be read in a way that was never intended.

Consider the extra steps people might take to make sure their messages are understood, and maintain their original meaning. Information might be turned into stories, songs, or rhymes to make them easier to remember. Historically, letters have had blank space crossed out to avoid anything extra being added to them. And personal seals, pressed into wax, added an extra layer of security. Receiving a letter with a broken seal, or an incorrect seal, the recipient would know that it had been opened. And I'm sure that many of us have added emojis to messages to try and convey tone of voice.

The methods of communication that are available to your characters determine how quickly, easily, and cheaply messages can travel. Therefore it also determines what kind of messages are sent. If postage and paper is very high cost, people are less likely to send personal or trivial communications. If, however, it's as easy as sending a message on your phone, people are likely to share far more than is actually necessary.

Cost, and access to technology may mean that different people have to use different methods. There may be some who can afford to send letters, while others have to settle for a conversation over the back fence.

In turn, this impacts other aspects of their lives: someone who is unable to send messages over long distances may prefer to set up home closer to their extended family. Someone who speaks only with those in their own town is less likely to know about the wider world, or have access to many different points of view. But remember that access to the world doesn't necessarily equate to a more informed, empathetic population. Online, people often create 'echo chambers' for themselves, surrounding themselves with a network of people with similar opinions and beliefs. A wider net of communication doesn't always give people a broader mind.

It may be that only some members of your population are able to write. Or are allowed to buy stamps. Or are able to use a telephone. Perhaps telephones require magical powers to work, or maybe they only connect after a citizen's ID number is inputted. Perhaps certain people's ID numbers are barred. Those with criminal records, or those who have spoken out against the government, or those in debt.

There may also be social barriers to communication. It may be considered immoral or shameful for an unmarried woman to have free access to a telephone. Typed communications might be considered rude, or only ever used for the most formal messages.

And also think about other conventions in your culture. Are reports of someone's death always delivered in a black envelope? Are love letters always carried by waterways, rather than roads? Is the arrival of the post a happy occasion, or a moment of trepidation? There may even be superstitions surrounding communication. Perhaps no one writes letters on a Thursday or uses a telephone at noon.

You can use communication to create some unique quirks in your society. But always remember to give them a purpose. How do they push the plot forward? How do they reveal character? How do they explore the themes of your book? Of course, you can add a quirk just because you like it, but it's even better if it plays a part in your story and your character's journey.

COMMON FORMS OF COMMUNICATION AND HOW THEY ARE USED:
BARRIERS AND INEQUALITIES TO USING COMMUNICATION:
LEGAL AND SOCIAL RESTRICTIONS ON COMMUNICATION:

FOOD

Food tends to be a hugely important part of any society. Of course, it's vital to life, but it's important for many other reasons too.

Opportunities for growing, rearing, and hunting food are major considerations when deciding where to establish communities. From popular camping spots, to farming towns, to sprawling cities. They need access to a varied food source in order to thrive. The availability of that food through the various seasons impacts trade, health, cooking practices, and food storage methods.

In turn, these create traditions and events: harvest festivals, feasts, the eating up of perishable foods, switching from fresh food to pickled, salted, and dried foods. It's no coincidence that we eat pancakes before lent, or eat dried fruit at Christmas. These are traditions that are born from practicalities of using up or preserving food when it's abundant, ready for the leaner months of the year. In modern life, these practices are no longer necessary, but they're retained as traditions nonetheless.

Also, traditions surrounding food have often been deeply rooted in expected gender roles. From the dawn of time, roles around hunting, gathering, cooking, and cleaning have been split down gender lines. They also tie into childcare, and the teaching of the next generation, as well as ideas of rites of passage and the transitions from childhood into adulthood. We still retain this today: for example, taking someone out for their first legal drink.

This is a perfect example of how one aspect of your world can impact, inform, and bleed into other areas. And it can impact even more of your culture: arranging school terms around harvests, allowing children to help on their parents' farms, arranging the working day around the demands of farming, and religious festivals that coincide with times food needs to be eaten up.

Perhaps magic utilises fruit, or blossom, or the fertility of the earth. Maybe magic is weaker in the winter, or maybe magic is relied on in the colder months in order to keep the population fed.

So far, we've talked about society-wide impacts of food, but it all comes down to a personal level too. What are the norms for family life? What are the ideals? Think about whether your families eat all together, or separately. Perhaps there are no set mealtimes, with people eating whenever they are hungry. Maybe mealtimes are strict, with minimal snacking between. Perhaps people eat communally, gathering together in the town hall to share food.

Whatever you decide, consider the whys. Why do people do it this way? It might be religious. It might be based on their norms and values, and the importance they put on family or community connectedness. If it's simply 'how they've always done it', there may be a practical reason hiding in your society's history.

A community plagued by vicious predators may have once protected itself with a ring of constantly burning fires. Those fires may have also been kept burning within homes, offering people an added sense of protection. It would, therefore, make sense to utilise those fires by keeping a pot of stew warm all day. Perhaps this is why people in your culture don't have set mealtimes and, while the predators have long-since been eradicated, the culture has remained, with people simply eating whenever they are hungry.

This lack of set mealtimes would also need to be reflected in the timetables of work and education. How would it affect cafés and restaurants? How would it affect relationships within families? How might it affect sleep patterns? Keep letting these questions bleed into the other parts of your world's culture and daily life, tying it all together to create a deep and believable world for your readers.

On the other hand, your characters might cram as many meals into the day as they can. Perhaps, due to years and years of past famine, it has become a marker of social status to eat more meals. It might be ingrained into your world's culture that, the more mealtimes you have, regardless of what or how much you eat, the 'posher' you are. Lower social classes often imitate the behaviour of those further up the social ladder. It's all a part of the *fake it 'til you make it* culture. *Keeping up with the Jones'*.

There's also a lot of polite and impolite behaviour surrounding food, such as not eating with your mouth full, or keeping your elbows off the table. These vary culture by culture, and become deeply ingrained in our behaviours. Some traditions will fall out of favour: we no longer, so commonly, stand when a lady stands up, and we're unlikely to be summoned to meals by the banging of a gong any more. (Although, as the owner of a gong, my dad does actually do this. Don't ask.) But many parents still refuse to let their children leave the table until everyone has finished, and reading at the table, or using a phone these days, is generally considered impolite by many. There are some cultures where you should never refuse food from your hosts, and others where you must never ask for salt or pepper.

There are also superstitions around food. Such as being the lucky one to find the sixpence in the Christmas pudding, or splitting the wishbone from the chicken. It may be unlucky to eat particular foods on particular days, or good luck to give away the crust of your pie (or your last Rolo).

In some cultures, it's rude to eat in public, in others it's a complete norm to eat with your hands. In some places the eldest will eat first, in others belching after a meal shows that you enjoyed it. Food traditions vary across the globe, so don't shy from creating some unique practices for your world.

At this point, bear in mind that food in your culture is inextricably linked to health and beauty standards. We're going to tackle these in a later chapter, but just have them in mind as you lay out your cultural norms surrounding food and eating.

USUAL MEALTIMES:
PRACTICALITIES/BELIEFS THAT HAVE CREATED THIS NORM:
WHERE THE IMPACT OF THIS IS SEEN IN LIFE:

HOW MEALTIMES HAPPEN (together, separately, communally, etc):
PRACTICALITIES/BELIEFS THAT HAVE CREATED THIS NORM:
WHERE THE IMPACT OF THIS IS SEEN IN LIFE:

FESTIVALS, FEASTS, SPECIAL MEALS:
PRACTICALITIES/BELIEFS THAT HAVE CREATED THIS:

IMPOLITE BEHAVIOUR WHILE EATING:
POLITE BEHAVIOUR WHILE EATING:
SUPERSTITIONS:
RITES OF PASSAGE:

LEISURE

Leisure is a luxury. When spending needs to be cut, it's the leisure that goes, leaving the essentials. It's also leisure time that disappears when a second or third job is taken on. The amount of leisure times someone has, and what they do with it, is a fascinating social measure.

So, while you're thinking about leisure in your world, keep this in mind: that people have different amounts of leisure time, and they have different amounts of disposable income to spend on it. And remember that it doesn't need to be a socio-economic distinction. Leisure can also be influenced by religion, education, location and ease of travel, the type of job someone does, their own personal values, physical ability, health and fitness. It might be impacted by social pressures and expectations: the fear of being judged, criticised, or ostracised. There may be legal restrictions, or magical ones.

First up, I want you to think about attitudes towards leisure in your world. Is it valued and protected? Or is it frowned upon as a self-indulgent waste of time? And how has this attitude come about?

It might be that your society is highly focussed on productivity, and leisure time is seen as lazy and selfish. But you can also analyse this further by taking another step back. Why is your society so focussed on productivity? Why does it value it above leisure? Perhaps your society is still recovering from war, and the labour force is much depleted meaning everyone has to work twice as hard to pull the country back to pre-war levels of production. Maybe, having recently won their independence from an empire, your society is working hard towards becoming fully self-sufficient.

On the flip-side, your culture might value leisure time above productivity. Perhaps self-care really does matter to your society, and leisure time is protected by law. Again, work your way back and decide *why* this is the case in your world's culture. Perhaps work unions fought for the rights of their people, pushing the government to pass laws for a better work/life balance. Maybe a mental health crisis destroyed the economy and put too much pressure on the health service as people took leave or left employment with stress-related problems. Maybe the government were forced to find a healthier work/life balance to get the country back on track. Perhaps a devastating natural disaster wiped out large numbers of the population and people began to re-evaluate their priorities. Maybe the culture-change came from the people, rather than from the top down.

Let's think about how people spend their leisure time. Remember that this will differ across your population, with the division based on a number of different factors such as wealth, physical ability, religion, age, and whether they live in the city or country.

A big decider for how leisure time is spent is the level of technology in your world. Do people have televisions and games consoles in their homes? Do they have bowling alleys, public swimming pools, and cinemas? Are there restaurants, golf courses, or health spas? Maybe children spend their time playing marbles, or learning to hunt, or doing needlework. Technology opens up many new options to your society, including the ability to travel greater distances at faster speeds.

Leisure activities will also be impacted by the things your society values most. Bear in mind that this will differ person to person, of course, but there are also general, overarching values that belong to the culture as a whole. In fact, many of our personal values will be influenced by our culture, whether we're aware of it or not. If you're unsure of your culture's main values, you can always skip forward to the Big Values chapter, or come back to this one later.

If your culture values health and fitness very highly, leisure time is more likely to be spent in active pursuits: team sports, hiking, swimming. Perhaps your culture greatly values the environment and being out in nature. Maybe it promotes quiet, reflective time alone, or places importance on family activities. Maybe it values knowledge, creativity, or beauty.

Another thing that influences leisure activities is the climate and topography your society experiences. Some activities may be hindered by poor weather, or be seasonal. There might be times that it's actually dangerous to be outdoors. Not many people will stay out in the rain for a barbecue or a picnic, except us Brits, but that's because we've had to get used to doing most things in the rain. It's part of our culture, influenced by our climate. See how it works?

Within an island community, most people will probably learn how to swim and fish. If your community live in the mountains they might all learn to ski and climb. In the city, leisure time might be spent in trendy coffee shops and art galleries, while the hub of a rural community might be the local pub or the post office. Perhaps your cities have vast, sprawling parks. Perhaps they have indoor skateparks and snow domes.

There may also be rules, whether formalised into laws, or unspoken, social rules, about who can and can't do certain things. There may be religious restrictions, banning believers from entering establishments that sell alcohol, or serve pork, or require the removal of gloves, or the sharing of shoes. There might be laws banning certain ethnic groups from places, segregating society. It might be considered shameful for women to gamble, or for children to ride horses, or for overweight people to swim. It's likely that certain activities will be age-restricted, such as drinking alcohol, gambling, or visiting a brothel. It's also likely that certain activities are outlawed entirely, such as recreational drugs, cock-fighting, or boxing.

And leisure activities are also restricted by socio-economic factors. As I stated at the beginning: leisure is a luxury, and not everyone can afford it; whether by money or time. How far, and how quickly, a family can afford to travel will impact their leisure choices. The technology they can afford in their home, the leisure equipment they can buy, the subscriptions and membership fees. Not everyone can afford a holiday home, or a hotel, or camping equipment. And not everyone can take holidays from their work, or afford to leave the business they run themselves.

GENERAL ATTITUDE TOWARDS LEISURE TIME:
HOW THIS IS REFLECTED IN EMPLOYMENT LAW:
HOW THIS WORK/LIFE BALANCE CAME ABOUT:

WHO HAS THE RIGHT TO A HEALTHY WORK/LIFE BALANCE?
WHO DOESN'T HAVE THESE RIGHTS?

COMMON LEISURE ACTIVITIES FOR ADULTS:
COMMON LEISURE ACTIVITIES FOR CHILDREN:

HOW THESE ARE INFLUENCED BY THE VALUES OF YOUR CULTURE:
HOW THESE ARE INFLUENCED BY CLIMATE AND TOPOGRAPHY:

LEISURE ACTIVITY RESTRICTIONS WRITTEN INTO LAW:
RESTRICTIONS BASED ON SOCIAL VALUES:
RELIGIOUS RESTRICTIONS:
WEALTH RESTRICTIONS:

HOLIDAYS

Closely related to leisure, is holidays. We have three specific definitions to think about here: how many days off are given by employment and education, public holidays as in festivities, and where people travel to on holiday or vacation, if you like. As ever, each of these will be impacted by and have an impact on the others.

For example, holidays from employment and education are often focused around certain festivals. Here in the UK, the school term gives holidays at both Easter and Christmas. Many businesses close over these times essentially enforcing days off, while other businesses have to retain staff on these days, often compensating by means of extra pay or time off in lieu.

Let's look at the first definition: the days off that people get from work and education. In many countries, the amount of days off is written into law. There may be laws about how many hours a day someone can work, or a week, or in a row, or how many night shifts they can work. These might be rules to maintain safety: such as with driving jobs, jobs that use heavy machinery, or jobs that require high levels of concentration.

But don't take those days off for granted! How did the worker earn that right? Diplomacy? Protest? Violence? Many employment rights have been hard won, and you can't take it for granted that they'll always exist, either. Employment rights in your world might be solid and secure, but they might be balancing on a knife's edge, ready to topple at any moment.

Let's move onto our second definition: festivities. Where are you going to place your major holidays? Are they based on seasons and climate, letting people out of their commitments for the best weather? Are they based on religious festivals? Or on the phases of the moon? Or on when people are needed for the harvest, or to battle the annual dragon migration? Are they based on magical rites of passage, or when the doorway to the spirit world stands ajar?

There may be public holidays to mark a specific historical event, either one that is celebrated as a high point in your world's history, or a more solemn occasion marked by sombre reflection or making amends. It might mark a great war victory, or the birth or death of a notable figure. It might be a memorial day on the anniversary of devastating natural disaster, or an invasion, or the death of a God.

Always bear in mind that these festivals may change over time. They may be commandeered by other groups or issues, their original meaning might be forgotten, misinterpreted, or their focus changed. As society changes over the years, some festivals may fall out of favour, and be re-evaluated as inappropriate. They might be outlawed in an effort to silence the people celebrating, or to ignore the issues they raise. Certain festivals may become more important over time, or less so. There may be festivals that no one remembers the origin of at all, simply celebrating them out of habit and tradition.

Now, let's jump to the final definition and look at where people travel to on their holidays, or what they might do. As with leisure time, this is very dependent on things like technology and your culture's values.

How far people can travel depends on whether they have to travel by horse and cart, or by car, high-speed train, or hyper-speed spaceship. Of course, they might travel by magic, or body-swapping, or morphatron probe transporter. But even within the available modes of travel, there are barriers to use. For example, not everyone can afford to have a morphatron probe transporter in their house. They might not even be able to afford to use the public ones with their slightly unreliable calibration.

In all seriousness, not everyone can afford a horse, let alone a ticket on the shiny new steam trains that rumble through the countryside. And there's the issue of logistics too. If you live 50 miles from the nearest train station, it adds an extra barrier to train travel. If your horse is elderly, or your cart can only carry two people, or if the space port is crawling with coalition factions and there's a warrant out for your arrest, it all adds extra complications and barriers. Some of which, are insurmountable.

Perhaps you can't afford to leave your farm for a holiday. Maybe you can't afford to miss the weekly markets. Perhaps your scholarship place requires school grades you're struggling to achieve. There are all kinds of concrete reasons that some people don't, or can't, go away on holiday.

There are also social barriers. Religious restrictions, personal values, societal expectations. These days, we might sneer at the idea of a 'booze cruise' or 'tourist traps'. We all have a fair idea of the kind of activities that might occur on an 18-30s holiday, or among football fans travelling to an away game abroad. Us Brits, in particular, have a pretty bad reputation for being loud, leery drunkards on holiday. So think about the kind of holiday behaviour that your culture might frown on. Are their holidays filled with sedate visits to museums and art galleries, or with drinking shots and getting tattoos they'll later regret?

Still, in a culture where they work incredibly hard, perhaps it's the expectation that they deserve to party hard too.

There may also be legal restrictions to travel. What kind of paperwork, licences, or agreements might your characters need in order to travel? How easy are they to obtain, and is everyone allowed to have them? Perhaps they're restricted to certain areas, or how many days they're allowed to be away from home. Maybe they can't obtain travel papers until they're 18 years old, or married, or employed full-time.

And consider where your citizens choose to travel for holidays, which will depend greatly on whether they're looking for relaxation, adventure, culture, or an adrenaline rush. People from a land-locked country might flock to the distant coast for a change of scenery, or they might be fearful of the water. People from a mountainous country might seek warmer, flatter landscapes, and those from arid, dry places, might seek out lush lakeside forests. Are your characters looking for a change, or do they prefer to stick to what they know? Maybe they're so fearful or suspicious of other countries and cultures that they never venture beyond their own borders.

Likewise, with the activities they choose to do while on holiday: are your people always up for a new challenge, or would they rather just relax and do as little as possible? Are they seeking out holidays that will fill them with excitement and adventure, or ones that will fill them with introspection and peace? Are they seeking out history and culture, or chasing the latest trends?

And, as ever, consider what barriers might stand in someone's way. Maybe someone wants to go llama trekking, but they're allergic to animals, or fearful of them. Perhaps your character desperately wants to go skiing, but the equipment is far too expensive. Or they want to experience light-speed travel, but their species are banned from it due to their tendency to vomit.

And take a moment to consider what your citizens are like when faced with an unfamiliar culture. Are they respectful and dignified, trying to avoid social faux pas, or do they shout when someone doesn't understand them, ignorantly pointing at what they want and stomping over their host's social norms. Are your people welcomed by other cultures, or do they have a reputation for behaving badly?

EMPLOYMENT LAW REGARDING DAYS OFF:
HOW WERE THESE EMPLOYMENT RIGHTS WON?

MAJOR HOLIDAYS:

HOLIDAY:
WHEN IS IT HELD?
WHAT DOES IT REPRESENT?
HOW IS IT CELEBRATED/MARKED?

HOLIDAY:
WHEN IS IT HELD?
WHAT DOES IT REPRESENT?
HOW IS IT CELEBRATED/MARKED?

HOLIDAY:
WHEN IS IT HELD?
WHAT DOES IT REPRESENT?
HOW IS IT CELEBRATED/MARKED?

HOLIDAY:
WHEN IS IT HELD?
WHAT DOES IT REPRESENT?
HOW IS IT CELEBRATED/MARKED?

ECONOMIC BARRIERS TO TRAVEL:
SOCIAL BARRIERS TO TRAVEL:
LEGAL BARRIERS TO TRAVEL:
POPULAR HOLIDAY DESTINATIONS:
POPULAR HOLIDAY ACTIVITIES:

MONEY AND WEALTH

Economics are complicated, and this isn't going to be all about the ins and outs of your economics system. The focus on this chapter is how money affects *people*. Their beliefs, their fears, their aspirations, the things they value. The way they value themselves.

While we all understand how capitalism works (to some extent, at least), we probably don't have much experience of any alternatives. Economic systems such as 'communism' and 'socialism' always get banded around as derogatory and cautionary buzz words, offered up as the inevitable outcome of voting this way, or that way. But they tend to be misinterpreted or misunderstood, and have largely lost their real meanings in the modern vernacular. They're little more than insults now.

But that's not to say you can't shift away from capitalism in your world. Or even create a better version of capitalism. Capitalism is, in its simplest terms, a system that seeks to make profit. That doesn't mean it needs to oppress, or become a glorified pyramid scheme. Or, you can create a world with aspects of capitalism, mixed with socialism (where the means of production are collectively owned), or economic democracy (democratic control of firms by their workers), or permaculture (an agriculturally productive system). You can give it a whole new name, a whole new philosophy, and a whole new outcome.

But every economic system requires consideration of three key components: first, the production of food and goods. Of everything your society needs. Second, the distribution of those goods, that food. From sharing eggs with your neighbour, or the collection of everything produced into a government redistribution system, to worldwide (or even galaxy-wide) logistics and shipping. And third, the consumption of goods. From the food we eat, to the clothes we wear, and the tech we use.

You already know what I'm going to say: how you decide these things are handled in your world will have an impact on the culture surrounding money and wealth. There will always be the 'haves' and the 'have-nots', whether the inequality is real and concrete, or just perceived and imagined through envious eyes. No matter what system you produce, however fair you try to make it, you're likely to have cries of "that's not fair!" from some of your citizens.

Let's hop back to capitalism for now, as it's a system we'll all understand. Everything in a capitalist society has a worth. Whether that be labour or the goods that labour produces. There is a cost, an exchange, a contract. And the worth of anything is in constant flux. It's a balanced see-saw, teetering between the seller and the buyer.

If you pay too little for labour, workers will work elsewhere. If you pay more, you eat into your own profits (which is, of course, the preoccupation of capitalism: to make a profit). If you pay your workers more, you have to raise the price of your goods to make back the shortfall in profit. But if you raise your prices too much, people will stop buying your goods. It's a fine balance. Of course, there are ways to tip the balance, by increasing the perceived value of your goods. By setting yourself up as a luxury brand, so that people *expect* to pay more, and are *willing* to pay more, especially if it raises their own social value. And people might pay more for goods that arrive faster, or that are easier to assemble, or goods that are more environmentally friendly, or align with their religious beliefs. But the balance of worth needs to be kept level, tweaking back and forth whenever it begins to tip.

Of course, there are also the things people *have* to buy. You can buy cheaper and cheaper food, but you can't easily stop altogether. Likewise with fuel, utilities, housing, healthcare.

There are countless sayings regarding money. From 'money makes the world go round', to 'money can't buy happiness', each expressing a cultural belief about money. It's interesting to pick them apart and really think about them: what beliefs are they encouraging? What behaviour are they excusing? And who's benefiting? Think about the kind of money sayings that might exist in your world.

Do beliefs around money encourage hard work and persistence? Do they encourage people to be happy with what they have, rather than striving for more?

Consider *how* people are thought to become wealthy in your world. What's the difference between a poor person and a rich person? Is wealth a case of hard work? Are people poor simply because they're lazy? Perhaps wealth is simply a case of good or bad luck. (To further that: are we pawns played by destiny, or do we make our own luck?) Perhaps wealthy people are chosen or blessed by God. Maybe they're more worthy, somehow.

I recognise a strange contradiction in my own culture: while wealth is the ultimate desire, wealthy people are often portrayed as bad guys. With characters like Scrooge and Cruella de Vil, and sayings about 'money being the root of all evil', it's a common and widespread belief that you can't be both rich and a good person. That money will corrupt even the saintliest of souls. Maybe it's a way to curb jealousy, maybe it's a way to suppress the desire for upwards social mobility. Maybe it's simply fun to vilify and pick fun at our superiors. But with money being such a necessity in our lives, and the cause of such hardship when it's in short supply, it's interesting to see how we commonly portray those who have it.

But perhaps, in the world you're creating, money isn't linked to evil at all. Perhaps it's synonymous with freedom, or generosity, or philanthropy. Maybe money is shared more equally, maybe it's less of a necessity, or perhaps it doesn't even exist at all. Perhaps wealth is thought of as a reward for intelligence, or beauty, or physical strength. Maybe it's seen as a result of oppression, or theft, or greed.

And perhaps there is no division between rich and poor. Maybe social mobility is encouraged and applauded, with those further up the ladder reaching down to help others ascend. Perhaps people can marry out of their class, or education offers every chance to every student, or hard work really does pay off, for everyone, every time. Maybe no one games the system, or has a head start.

But economics are a rich source for adding conflict into the lives of your characters, and used as a main theme in genres such as dystopian and cyberpunk. The disparity between rich and poor, the differences between what the two groups can and can't afford, and the separation in their quality of life is a rich source of division and conflict. It's a way to instantly create the much-loved underdog. It can give your character their goal, their purpose, and offer up countless barriers to them achieving it. It can be their catalyst to act, their turning point.

And the attitudes that people have about the poor, and the attitudes that people have about the rich, can say so much about your culture and the place money holds in it.

Can money, in your world, truly buy happiness?

GENERAL ATTITUDES TOWARDS MONEY AND WEALTH:
HOW THE POOR FEEL ABOUT THE WEALTHY:
HOW THE WEALTHY FEEL ABOUT THE POOR:
OPPORTUNITIES FOR SOCIAL MOBILITY:

DISTRIBUTION OF WEALTH:
SOME BELIEFS AND/OR SAYINGS ABOUT MONEY:

HOW WEALTH IMPACTS:

ACCESS TO EDUCATION:
CAREER OPTIONS:
HOME AND FAMILY SET-UP:
ACCESS TO HEALTHCARE:
ACCESS TO POSITIONS OF POWER:

CHARITY AND WELFARE

Let's take a look at people who need a little extra help in your society, and where that help comes from.

Charity can be given as money, or as goods (new or pre-used), or as time. Maybe, in your world, one is thought of as more noble, more worthy, than another.

Are charitable donations expected? Are they enforced? Perhaps it's dictated by religion, or political leaning, or used as a way to make amends for bad behaviour.

If charity is expected, or enforced, do people get a sense of fulfilment? Are they admired for their good work? If charity is required by law, it may be viewed as a tax, or attract feelings of bitterness or resentment. It may be viewed in a totally different way than if it's given willingly, and by choice.

And how are recipients of charity chosen? This can say a lot about your culture. There are countless charities out there, from those fighting to protect animals, to those seeking cures for cancer. Which are deemed most worthy? Which are the most popular to give to? Is your society made up of animal lovers, or are sick children their focus? It might be that they favour literacy programmes, or protecting historic buildings, or clothing the poor. Consider which charities are the most popular, and what that says about your culture. About where their sympathies lie. About who they pity.

Beyond charity as a way to help those in need, is there an organised welfare system? Are wages topped up with benefit payments? Are children provided for? Are the elderly given an income after retirement?

Is your culture a socialist one, seeking to raise everyone's quality of life, or are people left to sink or swim by themselves?

It might be that your culture seeks equality, and strives to flatten out any disparities. Or maybe they view the lack of welfare as a way to make people work harder, more ambitious. To toughen them up. Perhaps some people are seen as being worthy of welfare support, while others are viewed as lazy, expecting something for nothing.

Consider how easy it is for people in your world to slide from being self-sufficient to needing help. What happens if they are injured, or become sick? What happens if their work dries up, or the family's breadwinner is jailed, or if they lose everything they own in a fire? What happens when they become too old to work? What happens when they become pregnant, have young children to care for, or care for someone else?

There are so many reasons why someone would suddenly find themselves in need of welfare. Is there a system to help them? And, even if there is, are they eligible? Think about the criteria for someone receiving welfare support. Perhaps they need to have worked for a certain number of years, or have a certain level of education. Maybe they become ineligible if they break the law, if they refuse to follow the main religion, or if they become pregnant out of wedlock. There may be people who can't apply at all.

WHY DO PEOPLE GIVE TO CHARITY?
WHAT IS THOUGHT OF PEOPLE WHO GIVE TO CHARITY?
POPULAR CHARITABLE CAUSES:

WELFARE SYSTEM IN PLACE:
WHO IS ELIGIBLE FOR WELFARE SUPPORT?
WHO IS INELIGIBLE?

PATRIOTISM

The word 'patriot' exists in the same family of words as 'patriarch'; a collection based around the concept of 'father'. The fatherland. It came to the English language via the French word for 'fellow countryman', and began, almost instantly, to pick up the modifier 'good'. A good patriot was suddenly a concept, as opposed to a bad one. A good fellow countryman.

But the word, the concept, has a tumultuous time in our language and culture. Just as a good patriot can love their country, a good patriot can also be *too* patriotic. The idea is viewed with as many negative connotations as positive ones. Think about it for a moment. Think about how divisive a word it has become. A word that simply meant a 'fellow countryman' when it first arrived.

A person can be berated for being unpatriotic, but they can be berated for being too patriotic, for being a zealous patriot. It seems that there is a balance to be found. That one must strive to be just the right amount of patriotic. It's a fascinating take on a word, and shows how powerful, how dangerous, language can be.

But, enough word-nerding for now. Let's start thinking about what patriotism looks like in your fictional world.

If your world is currently at war, whether with another country or a civil war within its own borders, patriotism is likely to look very different to a world during times of peace. Patriotism might be enlisting to fight, it might be turning your garden over to growing vegetables, it might be giving your home up to the military. Patriotism might be reporting your neighbours to the authorities, it might be burning the homes of conscientious objectors, it might mean shooting them.

Also, consider the implications if a character is viewed to be 'unpatriotic'. Perhaps they're expected to house and care for a wounded soldier. Perhaps that soldier is to be given half of the family's rations. Perhaps he's to be given the medicine they need for their child. Medicine that is in very short supply. Maybe he gets an eye for their young daughter. What happens if they refuse to let him stay? Are they shunned? Are they shot?

Remember that the consequences for unpatriotic behaviour would come from both the authorities and the community. Maybe the community is sympathetic, and rally around to help. Perhaps the authorities simply shrug and move on while the community choose to ostracize the family. The implications may be completely different. They may be entirely opposite, and they may be wholly unexpected.

In times of peace (or relative or perceived peace), the idea of patriotism is probably completely different. It might look more like voting in elections, supporting sports teams, buying local produce, or picking up litter in the street. Pride in where someone lives often starts small, with the immediate area around them.

These are examples of quiet, personal, often unseen patriotism. But patriotism might be more vocal and present. It might mean children singing the national anthem each day in school, or the flying of flags on public buildings, or photographs of the monarchy in every home.

There may be rewards for patriotic behaviour. Medals, awards, public recognition. Perhaps lower taxes, cheaper rent, or promotions at work. How is loyalty to the country rewarded, and who decides on the recipients of those rewards?

There may even be laws regarding patriotism. Perhaps it's a legal requirement to raise a flag on your house every day. It might be a legal requirement to vote, or to recite a pledge to your country each day at work, or to donate a portion of your wages to charity. Patriotism isn't always freely given.

As we've already considered, patriotism can also go too far. What might that look like in your world? Dragging perceived traitors onto the streets for a beating, xenophobic and racist attacks, hooliganism and vandalism at sporting events.

But it doesn't have to appear as violence. It might be secretly informing on people in the community, or shunning those with different values. It might be harmful to the zealot themselves: obeying the authorities to a detrimental extent, isolating themselves, putting themselves in dangerous situations.

As ever, keep bringing it back to your characters. How patriotic are they? Do they feel that their country is worthy of their love and loyalty? There are plenty of chances here for conflict, for inciting incidents and turning points in your character's journey.

WHAT IS EXPECTED OF THE PATRIOTIC:

IN TIMES OF WAR:
IN TIMES OF PEACE:

CONSEQUENCES FOR UNPATRIOTIC BEHAVIOUR IN TIMES OF WAR:
CONSEQUENCES FOR UNPATRIOTIC BEHAVIOUR IN TIMES OF PEACE:
WHAT ARE THE REWARDS FOR PATRIOTIC BEHAVIOUR?

LEGALLY REQUIRED PATRIOTISM:
EXAMPLES OF EXTREME PATRIOTISM:

DIVERSITY

Let's consider diversity in your world. How different are people? And are their differences evident, are they adapted for, are they even legal?

We recognise an expanding list of personal characteristics, both primary (such as age, ethnicity, gender, sexuality, mental and physical ability) and secondary (such as nationality, education, income, religion, work experience, geographic location, marital status). Of course, when you add in a fantasy element, you can increase these lists to include things such as species or magical ability.

The amount of inclusion and adaptions that are made in your world, the way in which diversity is viewed, accepted, and embraced is likely to be in constant flux. And, despite the presence of legislation and expectations, the treatment of diversity across your populace is likely to be as diverse as the diversity itself. As society changes over time, attitudes will change, as will the laws.

Diversity may not be particularly evident in your world. There are certain characteristics that are able to be concealed and kept private, while others can't be. On the other hand, your society might be openly diverse, with differences on clear display. Diversity may be shameful, unaccepted, or illegal, or it might be celebrated, admired, and protected by law.

But it may not be a blanket one or the other. There might be some diverse characteristics that are accepted (even if not in private), adapted for, and protected, while others are frowned upon, discriminated against, or legislated against. Such examples may come from both the primary and secondary characteristics categories.

You might have a world that accepts physical disability but denies learning difficulties. It might fully accept diverse ethnicities, yet discriminate against unmarried people. It might help out poor people in the city while leaving the poor in rural locations to fend for themselves. It might appear to make no sense at all.

So, how do you decide? You have two places to look: one is the rest of your culture and the set-up of your world, and the other is your character's story.

A country that was once violently invaded by another might hold onto a deep-rooted fear, mistrust, or hatred of people of that ethnic origin. A country that is deeply religious might hold onto the prejudices and judgements written into their religious texts. A country that was ripped apart by magic might discriminate against the portion of the populace that have (or used to have) magical abilities. A country that has learnt a harsh lesson might embrace diversity, making laws to encourage and promote it.

And diversity is something that can tie into your character's story. Perhaps they're the victim of discrimination, or someone they love is. Maybe they're actively fighting to change attitudes, to change the law. Discrimination against them might be a catalyst for action, or a barrier in them reaching their goal. Equally, their prejudice against someone else might cause them conflict. Rivals teaming up is a popular trope to play with. Two cultural enemies forced to work together to get what they want.

You can, carefully, use your fiction to highlight injustice in the real world, to explore themes of discrimination, or offer a path to greater equality. Of course, you want to avoid giving a moral lecture to your readers, but fiction is a powerful tool for exploring issues in the real world, especially when transported into a fantastical setting.

DIVERSITY EVIDENT IN YOUR WORLD:
CONCEALED DIVERSITY:
LAWS TO PROTECT DIVERSE CHARACTERISTICS:
LAWS AGAINST DIVERSE CHARACTERISTICS:
CULTURAL PREJUDICE:

INTEGRATION AND EXCLUSION

Now that you've decided on the diversity that exists in your world, let's drill right down into the treatment of that diversity.

Remember when we talked about charity? I said that the charities that are popular say a lot about your society: the things they value, the people they deem worthy, the ones they pity. And you can draw on those things again to explore how your culture treats people with diverse backgrounds and characteristics. Which they seek to accommodate for, which have a degree of equality, and which are still striving for recognition.

Who is welcomed into your society? Who is expected to integrate, with the onus put on them with no allowances made? Who is outright excluded? Denied equality or recognition? Even, denied access altogether?

Maybe you have a culture with gender equality, for the binary, or beyond, but also has extreme prejudice against older people. Perhaps your society is fully adapted for those with physical abilities, but dismisses learning difficulties and mental health issues as witchcraft. Your culture might fully accept different sexualities, but believes people with freckles to be unnatural and evil. Or people with green eyes. Or people who are left handed.

You can choose something seemingly trivial or absurd as a prejudice. This kind of discrimination has happened throughout the world and throughout history. Such views are still maintained by some.

Bring it back to your character and their journey. What conflict can you create for them? Can you stop them from achieving their goal? Can you force them to overcome their own biases? Can they help make their culture a more accepting place? Can they learn to love themselves and their differences?

And remember that there is more to inclusion and exclusion than equality legislation. Always keep in mind that not everyone will hold the same views, regardless of any laws in place. And some people will break those laws, willingly and knowingly, to stay true to their own beliefs.

And while the law might sway one way on an issue, the general consensus of their culture might swing the other way entirely. Change isn't always easy, and creating a law is one thing, but changing a cultural norm is an entirely different thing altogether. It's not always easy to change people's minds, especially when they're culturally ingrained.

How does your culture treat immigrants? Are they accepted, or are they locked up, or turned away? And consider how different kinds of migrants might be treated differently: refugees, economic migrants, those with sought-after skills, those unable to speak the language. Women, children, single young men. Just as diverse as migrants are, so are the ways in which they might be viewed.

What about those who have broken the law? Are they given a fair chance at rehabilitation, a chance to right their wrong? Does your culture believe in second chances for everyone, or does it depend on the crime they committed, or how many times they've broken the law? What happens to those people who are viewed as irredeemable?

Perhaps it depends on how long their sentence was, or if the victims feel that justice has been served. Maybe they need to show remorse, or prove that they can be trusted.

What happens when someone goes against societal norms or expectations? It may be as simple as a woman visiting a swimming pool, or a child of a particular ethnic origin attending a certain school. It might be a couple having a child out of wedlock, or parents choosing to keep a disabled child. When someone breaks a norm, even if it's done with good intentions, as a stand against injustice, or if it's an act of pure love, there will be repercussions.

It might be acceptance. They may be applauded widely, and perhaps society adapts its views to accommodate new norms. Or it might be shaming. Shunning. Anything from rolled eyes and tutting, to bullying, ostracisation, or a true, physical threat to life. Breaking a societal norm might be a cheeky, rebellious act, or it might be putting one's life on the line.

There may be legal repercussions, if breaking that norm also meant breaking the law. Society might disagree, rallying behind the rebel, protesting and rioting. Fighting for change. Or, society might inflict a far worse, swifter punishment.

What happens to those who have been excluded from society? Can they survive alone? In primitive societies, exclusion from the tribe almost certainly resulted, eventually, in death. There truly was safety in numbers. What happens to those excluded from your society? Can they stay where they are, or are they forced to move away? Change their name, hide their past? Perhaps they're welcomed into an alternative sub-community. Maybe they can find a new tribe. Maybe they're left to wander alone, ignored, until they can either redeem themselves, or they give up trying.

As ever, how does this tie into your character's journey? Is their ostracisation their turning point? The catalyst for their adventure? It might be the best thing that's ever happened to them, freeing them from a strict set of values they disagree with (or that disagree with them). It might force them to re-evaluate their views, as they seek re-integration.

Perhaps it leads them to a fight to build a better, more accepting world.

WHO IS FULLY WELCOMED?
WHO IS EXPECTED TO MAKE ADJUSTMENTS AND INTEGRATE THEMSELVES?
WHO IS STILL STRIVING FOR ACCEPTANCE?
HOW DOES PUBLIC OPINION DIFFER FROM THE LAW?

WHAT BEHAVIOUR WILL RESULT IN EXCLUSION FROM SOCIETY?
IS THERE A CHANCE OF REDEMPTION?

NEWS AND THE SPREAD OF INFORMATION

We've already looked at the informal spread of information and gossip, so you'll already have a good idea of the different communication channels in your world; be that oral communication, written, digital, or even telepathic.

Now, let's look at how information is formally spread to your people.

Formal news and information may well use the same lines as gossip, but remember that this might cause misinformation to spread, or create a blockage in communication. If formal news is simply passed from one mouth to another, people may well misinterpret, forget details, or make mistakes, corrupting the information from its original form. People might add their own slants and prejudices, mixing their own opinions with facts, or turning news to propaganda, whether intentionally or not.

It's an unreliable way to distribute formal information and news, full of flaws and inadequacies. But that isn't to say that any other method is flawless or less prone to prejudice and exploitation.

Perhaps there are written publications. Maybe everyone can read them, but maybe not. They might be read out by heralds or town criers, religious leaders or civil leaders, people who are expected, and trusted, to read the source material as it's written.

Maybe news reports are played on large screens mounted in public squares. Maybe they're beamed into every home, or broadcast to every device. Perhaps watching them is compulsory.

Is there a single news source, or several competing ones? Perhaps they have different focuses, preoccupations, and audiences. Maybe they have different allegiances, biases, funding sources. Are they trustworthy, or do they simply regurgitate propaganda without question?

Is the news subject to regulation and inspection? Perhaps there is an official ombudsman, or regular audits to ensure impartiality. Maybe the media have a self-regulatory code of conduct.

The news may be controlled, entirely, by the government. Independent news sources might be outlawed, with equipment seized and reporters jailed. Perhaps the news is controlled by the main religion, or by an educational institution, or by a magical society. Perhaps it's controlled by the military, or by the wealthy.

It might be freely owned by the people, open to public scrutiny, or collectively organised. Maybe it's entirely impartial, free from sensationalism, and run not for profit. Perhaps it's the pride of your nation: a completely free, trustworthy news source, unsullied and uninfluenced.

Do people look forward to hearing the news? When the herald's horn is blown, do they gather round eagerly, keen to hear the bulletin? Or is it a source of anxiety and trepidation? Perhaps it leans towards optimism, perhaps it prefers a pessimistic outlook.

Consider how present the news is in people's lives. Are they bombarded by it, required to hear it, enthralled by it? Perhaps they avoid it, or try to. Just how easy is it to avoid?

And consider the part news plays in your story. Perhaps it broadcasts your character's face, urging people to find them. Perhaps it publishes lies about your character, or about someone they love. Maybe your character seeks to uncover the truth beyond the lies that are broadcast as fact.

Maybe the news sources suddenly switch their allegiance. Maybe there's an information leak that turns the whole world on its head. Maybe, suddenly, the news channels fall completely silent, leaving society in the dark.

HOW IS NEWS BROADCAST?
HOW MANY NEWS SOURCES ARE THERE?
WHO CONTROLS THE NEWS?
HOW TRUSTWORTHY IS THE NEWS?

SECRETS, LIES, AND CONSPIRACIES

Not everyone trusts the government. Not all governments are trustworthy. Perhaps yours is, perhaps it isn't. Opinion is likely to be split regardless.

Secrets, lies, and conspiracies aren't a modern invention. Whether those in charge are doing it to keep peace, to protect their people, or to benefit their own interests, secrets have always been kept. Lies have always been told. And conspiracy theories have always arisen.

It may be that your government is lying about something that happened in the past. Perhaps they're covering up shameful acts. Perhaps they're glorifying history, and making themselves out to be the good guys while vilifying others. Maybe they're claiming a victory they never had, or taking the glory for something they never invented, or maybe they're, quite literally, hiding skeletons in their closets.

There may be secret agencies spying on their people, or involving themselves in foreign politics, or trying to control public opinion. Maybe they're keeping the existence of monsters a secret, or the existence of magic, or they're searching for a child mentioned in an ancient prophecy. Maybe they're *really* doing it for the public's own good or, at the very least, truly believe so.

If you're delving into the dystopian or urban fantasy genres, this is an important place for you to linger. Dystopian worlds often include corrupt and secretive governments, and urban fantasy often has a secret or hidden paranormal world existing alongside humanity.

Consider how trustworthy your leaders are. Are they altruistic and forthright, or are they cagey and deceitful? The actual honesty of your government might not be reflected in public opinion. They may be beloved and commended, but be hardly worthy of the accolade. Alternatively, they might be despised and doubted, when they are truly upfront and dependable. Perhaps they're skilled at PR, promoting themselves as far better than they are. Perhaps they're carrying the burden of judgement because of a previous authority who were less than trustworthy.

Think about the secrets your government might be keeping, or the lies they might be telling. What are their reasons? Self-interest, or public protection? Who benefits from their lies, and who suffers because of them?

Think, carefully, about the impact of the secrets that are being kept, and think about the impact the truth would have, should it be uncovered. How keen are the government to protect their secrets? To what lengths would they go to protect them?

One way in which secrets are protected is by discrediting those trying to uncover the truth. They're often depicted as crazy, obsessive, lunatics. They may, in fact, find themselves locked up in an asylum to keep them silent. They might find that their life is in danger. Do they have to go into hiding? Protect their identity? Who's willing to go further: those keeping the secrets, or those trying to uncover them?

What conspiracy theories exist in your world? Maybe they're spot on. Maybe they're absolute nonsense. Perhaps they're close to the truth, but not quite there yet. How are these theories shared, and what's thought about the people who investigate them? How successful has the smear campaign against them been? How close are they to uncovering the truth?

HOW TRUSTWORTHY IS YOUR GOVERNMENT?
WHAT IS THE PUBLIC'S OPINION OF THEM?
LIES YOUR GOVERNMENT ARE TELLING:
THE IMPACT OF THESE LIES:
CONSPIRACY THEORIES IN YOUR WORLD:

THE BIG VALUES

The big values of your culture are so important. They reveal so much. They're the culmination of all the work you've done so far.

They're a tell-all about your society, as well as being a guide map for your characters.

Think about the elements of culture that you've already created: attitudes towards the arts and creativity, traditions around food, thoughts about money and charity, diversity in your culture. Think about all of that, and consider what values might have created a society that functions in such a way. Likewise, consider what values would form in that kind of society.

What personality traits are valued? Perhaps your culture admires conscientiousness and productivity. Perhaps it admires politeness and obedience. It might view rest as laziness, and indulging in hobbies as selfishness. Maybe the traits that are valued serve industry and support employers.

Maybe your culture is deeply religious, and values honesty, piety, and humbleness. Maybe it values submission, self sacrifice, and discipline. Perhaps honesty, kindness, and generosity.

Perhaps your culture seeks to create a military force the rest of the world fear to stand against, valuing strength, ruthlessness, leadership. Maybe nobleness, comradeship, and dependability.

Your culture might view a quick temper as weakness, while admiring crying as a sign of passion. It might see compassion as being foolish, and indifference as prudent. Maybe it views chatter and noisiness as decadence, while seeing silence as virtuous.

Also consider whether the traits that are valued tend to be associated with a particular gender, such as strength, independence, and ambition versus compassion, gentleness, and affection.

How is this preference for certain traits reflected in society? What kind of people are elected to govern? What kind of people get the top jobs? Which traits are encouraged and which are shamed and reproached out of a child's behaviour? Think about how these traits are encouraged through the education system, or seen in rewards in the workplace. How is the bias evident in how children are raised, and the activities people partake in in their leisure time?

The personality traits that are valued don't exist in isolation. They are informed by other aspects of your culture, just as they, themselves, impact other parts of your society. The personality traits that are admired will match the overall goals of your people.
If one of the main goals in your population is the accumulation of wealth, they are

likely to value ambition, or diligence, or thriftiness. If one of the main goals is devotion to God, they may well value honesty, or loyalty, or authoritarianism. If it's education and intellectual enlightenment, they might value studiousness, or curiosity, or creativity.

When certain traits are seen as better, as more valuable, as more useful, it means that certain people are viewed as better, as more valuable, as more useful. It means that certain people are glorified, and seen as shining examples, while others are viewed as failing, or less-than. How is this reflected in the way they're treated, and the life chances they're given? Are those with lesser traits viewed as a burden, or as needing re-education, or as lost causes? Are those with admired traits given extra leeway, their flaws overlooked, their mistakes brushed off? Are they allowed to get away with more bad behaviour because of their perceived value to society?

WHICH PERSONALITY TRAITS ARE VALUED?
WHICH PERSONALITY TRAITS ARE DISLIKED?
HOW ARE THESE PREFERENCES SEEN IN SOCIETY?
HOW DO VALUED TRAITS FEED INTO LIFE GOALS?
HOW ARE THOSE WITH VALUED/UNVALUED TRAITS TREATED DIFFERENTLY?

EXPECTATIONS AND NORMS

What does your society expect of its people? What do the authorities expect of them? What do citizens expect of one another?

Expectations will begin from a very young age. The expectation that children obey their parents. That they learn right from wrong. That they work hard at school. That they don't swear, or drink, or have sex.

There will be expectations in the workplace: respect your boss, be polite to customers, turn up on time and don't leave early. Expectations at home: clean up after yourself, brush your teeth, don't hit your partner. There are expectations in general society: don't be violent, don't spit in the street, wear clothes, respect your elders.

Some expectations are formal: laid out in laws, written into contracts or codes of conduct, or existing in religious texts. Other expectations are informal and policed by your peers. There are expectations that our parents teach us, that we learn through experience, or that exist as part of our moral understanding of right and wrong. And there are expectations that remain entirely unspoken.

Your culture might expect your citizens to be law-abiding, hard-working, and obedient. It might expect them to be kind, to give to charity, and to help strangers. Maybe it expects them to invite those strangers into their homes, to feed and clothe them, to find them work or medical attention. Your culture might have perfectly reasonable requests, or it might go a little too far in what it expects.

It might expect chastity, virginity, or reproduction on a large scale. It might expect unquestioning devotion to the crown, for citizens to enlist in the military, or for farmers to hand over half their harvest to the authorities.

But just as your culture expects things of its citizens, your citizens, in return, have expectations of their own. There are things that they expect from their government.

They might expect safety and security. Perhaps free healthcare and education, or financial support if they fall on hard times. They might expect a job, a home, a partner. Access to clean water, or religious protections, or access to magical instruction.

More informally, people will expect something of one another. They might expect their fellow citizens to be friendly, courteous, and reliable. They might expect them to be moral, honest, and upstanding. Perhaps they expect their fellow citizens to think and act very similarly to themselves. This, of course, is probably a little too much to expect.

Most expectations come with punishments for stepping out of line. These might be a scolding, a roll of the eyes, a tut. It might be detention, a slap on the hand, extra homework. Perhaps a cut in wages, missing out on a promotion, or losing your job. Or it may be prison, a public whipping, or banishment from the city.

If someone breaks from what their government expects of them, it might see them excluded from certain freedoms, benefits, or responsibilities. They may no longer be able to vote, or leave their house after dark, keep animals, or hold a position of power.

Perhaps they lose their rights to education, or their library card, or access to the local post office. Maybe they're barred from a pub, or thrown our of their rental property, or have their children removed.

Just as there are many varied expectations that they could deviate from, there are just as many consequences for doing so.

Of course, it might be that their rebellion starts a movement. That it forces a change in attitude, a change in procedure, or even a change in the law. Your characters might be trailblazers, they might be champions, they might be heroes. They could change society for the better, as long as they're brave enough to face the consequences.

WHAT DOES YOUR CULTURE EXPECT OF ITS CITIZENS?

HOW IS THIS SEEN IN TERMS OF:

THE LAW:
RELIGION:
EDUCATION:

EMPLOYMENT:
GENERAL SOCIETY:

WHAT DO THE PEOPLE EXPECT FROM THE GOVERNMENT?

WHAT HAPPENS WHEN PEOPLE DON'T DO WHAT IS EXPECTED OF THEM?
WHAT HAPPENS WHEN THE GOVERNMENT DOESN'T DO WHAT PEOPLE EXPECT OF THEM?

The close cousin of expectations, is norms. It is the behaviour which society sees as 'normal'. It's the benchmark of ordinary, and the point at which nothing surprises. It comes from the Latin word *norma,* meaning precept, rule, or carpenter's square. It's the measure from which normality (and, by proxy, abnormality) is measured.

Norms are measured against the entire spectrum of life choices. It might be the norm for someone's life plan to look a little like this:

birth → school → college → university → job → marriage → mortgage → children

But what happens when that norm is broken? It could be broken by choice: choosing not to go to university, choosing not to settle down but to travel the world in a canoe. Alternatively, it could be broken by circumstance: not getting the grades needed for university, a housing crisis, disease, accidents, infertility, or early death.

When someone looks at the character choosing life in a canoe, they might raise their eyebrows and shake their head. They might gossip about how irresponsible they are, how selfish, how immature.

Ask yourself, why might someone see such a life choice as selfish? Because it doesn't follow the norms, therefore, it doesn't follow the expectations. Expectations are wrapped up in duties and responsibilities: a duty to work and pay your taxes, a duty to be a good consumer, a duty to provide the next generation of work force.

So what about circumstances? What about things we didn't actively choose? Often, the result is pity. "It's so sad they didn't manage this or that." "It's so sad that they never got the chance to fulfil their potential." What's their potential? The norms and expectations laid out in their culture.

The circumstance that takes you outside the set norms might be one of your personal characteristics: your skin colour, your hair colour, your sexuality, your physical ability, your mental health. Things you can't change about yourself (although some will debate that). While someone can retake exams or seek fertility treatment, or adopt, or wait for a better housing market, there are some things about yourself you cannot change (although, with future technology, who knows?)

Even when the norm you've broken is entirely out of your control, there might still be consequences. And the consequence for stepping outside the norms might be more than rolled eyes and shaken heads. It might mean bullying (both physical and emotional), it might mean campaigns of hate. Someone's position as part of a community might become impossible. Their very existence might be seen as a threat, as an attack on the culture, or it may even be illegal.

On the other side of the coin, of course, there are times that stepping out of the norms is celebrated. Just as with breaking expectations, sometimes breaking norms is celebrated. Sometimes it can change long-held views, break down prejudice, or change the order of the world entirely.

So when you're thinking about expectations in society, also think about the norms. They're so closely related, so tied together. Arguably, they might be largely the same.

And think about where the norms stem from. Who sets the benchmark for normality? And what does the benchmark tell us about the culture and the society? What does it tell us about the preoccupations and goals of that culture?

And think: whose goals are they?

MORALITY

Lessons in morality start in infancy. Don't tell lies. Don't snatch. Don't hit people. We begin understanding the difference between right and wrong before we even take our first steps.

Morality can be self-governing, and it probably is most of the time. We don't steal that chocolate bar because of the fear of outside consequences—the police, our parents—but most of us won't steal that chocolate bar because we inherently understand that it's wrong. We're not that kind of person.

Of course, we all know that nothing in life (or in worldbuilding) is that black and white. We all view someone who steals a chocolate bar, or a pair of jeans, or a widescreen TV as being very different to the person who steals a sandwich because they're starving. Likewise, we view someone stealing from a supermarket very differently to one who breaks into a house, or snatches a handbag in the street. Morality is never black and white, even if the law tries to make it so.

Building on everything you've created in your culture so far, let's start thinking about all those rules of morality. The dos and don'ts of your culture.

Of course, morality is entirely subjective. It depends on so much: your upbringing, your childhood influences, your experiences with religion, or the police. It is coloured by your view of big corporations and the government, and how honest or corrupt you believe them to be. It is impacted by the sentiment of "well, if they can do it, why can't I?" It also depends on how afraid you are of getting arrested, or punished by your parents. It depends on how desperately you need to keep hold of your job or reputation.

In stories, morality can be a fantastic source of conflict. You can cause your characters internal conflict by having them face a moral dilemma. By standing their own sense of right and wrong in the way of them achieving their ultimate goal. They might be split between two different moral codes, such as their own, and that of their religion. You can also partner them with someone who's sense of morality is different to their own, and have them face a dilemma where they disagree on the moral question. And, of course, you can bring them up against an antagonist with a different sense of morality.

The antagonist option is always one with interesting avenues to explore, as these are characters that require their own backstory, and they're frequently shown to be morally grey characters, rather than being straight up 'evil'. That they're acting out of good intentions, or believe they're doing the right thing. Of course, the antagonist doesn't need to be a solitary person; it can be a corporation, a government, or a community.

So, let's get back to the morals that exist in your fictional culture. You'll have the big fundamental ones such as don't murder people, and don't steal, and don't set fire to things. The big morality items are usually laid out in the laws. But always remember that things aren't always so simple. For example, it might be legal to kill another person as part of a sporting tournament, or in a duel. It might be legal if they are threatening your family, or your livestock, or if they walk over the graves of your ancestors.

There may also be things that are, technically, illegal, but are very unlikely to result in any punishment. Things that the authorities will overlook due to the circumstances. Such as euthanasia, or stealing out of necessity, or family matters, or the settling of a feud through equal retaliation.

Beyond the wriggle-room here, also consider whether moral standards are equally applied to everyone. It might be that women are held to different moral standards than men, or that elderly people have different moral guidelines. Perhaps it is split by religion or ethnicity. Perhaps by social status, or wealth, or job role.

Those working to uphold the standards of morality (such as police officers, judges, or religious leaders) are often expected to be an example to others, to be more immune to corruption. Consequently, if they do break the law, they may be punished more harshly under the understanding that 'they should know better', that they abused their position. They also activated the "if they can do it, why can't I?" question, potentially pulling down the moral structure of those around them.

There may be other ways in which the consequences are unfairly issued. Perhaps poor people receive harsher punishments, or certain ethnicities, or species. People of a certain religion, or sexuality, or magical ability.

And, again, remember that some moral issues are handled by the legal authorities. Some might be handled by a town elder or a council. Others by religious leaders or groups. Others by parents. And others by the communities in which the characters live. And the consequences might range from public whippings or walks of shame, to tuts and gossip. But remember that, in some circumstances, in some stories, the gossip might just be worse than the whipping.

Also remember that moral codes change over time. As the world, and your culture, changes and evolves, so does that sense of morality by which people govern their lives. Following an apocalypse, stealing and killing may quickly become acceptable. It might become an 'anything goes' culture just in order to survive. Things that were unacceptable to an older generation, might not hold any shame at all to younger people, such as sex before marriage, swearing, or having a baby out of wedlock. Maybe the morality around black magic becomes a little grey. Perhaps advances in technology push morality changes through society.

The changes might happen slowly, generation by generation, allowing people to (relatively) easily adapt and change to them. Maybe they happen suddenly, causing outrage and shock, causing people to rebel and fight back. Maybe morality in your culture is strict, and governs every action, with swift and harsh punishments.

Maybe the moral code is loose and always in flux, flowing like a gentle river through the generations, allowing people to define their own lives without shame or judgement.

MORALITY GOVERNED BY THE LAW:
MORALITY GOVERNED BY RELIGION:
MORALITY GOVERNED BY SOCIETY:
INEQUALITIES IN MORAL EXPECTATIONS:
INEQUALITIES IN CONSEQUENCES:
HOW MORAL CODES HAVE CHANGED OVER TIME:

ASPIRATIONS AND GOALS

What do people want? What do they strive for? As authors, we know all about goals for our characters; they should be striving for something in every scene. But what about their cultural aspirations and goals? What do people in their society generally strive for?

It might be wealth. It might be the big house with a front lawn and a picket fence. It might be the perfect family. These are the kinds of aspirations we see in Western culture, and it's reflected in education, employment, religion, family values, and the encouragement of norms. From a very young age (playing house) we're pushed towards these goals with encouragement from every part of society. We're told that these are the goals in life, and they become our goals.

But what about in your world's culture? The aspirations may be entirely different. Maybe they aspire to die in battle. Perhaps their names are exalted for all eternity, perhaps their families are richly rewarded for generations to come, perhaps it's the only route into paradise after they die.

Maybe the ultimate goal is to master the highest form of magic. Perhaps academic education is sidelined in preference of magic. Maybe those showing talent are removed from their communities and relocated in a shining city where they're surrounded, only, by other people working towards the same goal.

Of course, the ultimate goal might simply be day-to-day survival. They may not be able to aspire to things ten years in the future when all of their energy is spent on simply making it through that single day. It all depends on what life is like in your world.

But remember to reflect these aspirations in every aspect of your culture. People work towards these big life goals every single day, in everything they do, and this should be evident in every part of your world.

Of course, not everyone will subscribe to the big goals of your culture. There will be people who simply want something different from life, despite the cultural imprinting that happens throughout our lives. And there will be those who purposefully rebel against those aspirations. Not everyone wants a picket fence.

And while some people in your culture might have the money, the freedom, the opportunity to strive for those aspirations, others may be too wrapped up in wondering where their next meal is coming from. Although, they may still look longingly at the big houses and the tidy gardens.

Also, the expected goals encouraged by those in charge might be a smoke-screen, they might be a distraction. While people are dreaming about big houses, they might not notice that children with psychic powers are being quietly removed from their families. While people are working hard to get that promotion, they might not notice the rapidly expanding slums at the edges of the city. While people are searching, desperately, for 'the one', they might not notice that fewer and fewer children are being born.

And consider how those big goals have changed over time. In times of war, in times of famine, as well as in times of peace and plenty. The things we aspire to are as affected by our lives as our lives are affected by what we aspire to.

THE BIG LIFE GOALS AND ASPIRATIONS:

HOW ARE THESE ENCOURAGED THROUGH:

CHILDREN'S TOYS AND GAMES:
EDUCATION:
EMPLOYMENT:
RELIGION:
EXPECTATIONS AND NORMS:

SUPERSTITIONS

Superstitions are the offspring of beliefs. Beliefs can become deeply rooted in a culture and, in turn, become deeply embedded in its people and the way they see the world. They can cling on, even when they're no longer relevant. Even when they're proven to be false.

Beliefs range from big, important, fundamental understandings of the world, right down to inconsequential, trivial beliefs. Such as toast being a breakfast thing, and not to be eaten at any other time of the day.

But these beliefs come from somewhere.

Perhaps your country suffered several years of crop failures, forcing them to import food at great expense. Maybe bread became a luxury, not to be eaten more than once a day, simply because most people couldn't afford to. Or maybe widespread disease in cattle forced people to cut expensive meat from their diets. Perhaps bread became plentiful and cheap as farmers ploughed and planted on their grazing land. Perhaps the people became tired of eating it, and restricted themselves to having it once a day out of boredom. Several generations later, despite it having become irrelevant, perhaps the beliefs remain.

Beliefs can be stubborn and difficult to shift, even once they've become nothing more than habit, with the necessity of them long passed.

It might be that, as people forget the real reason, the practical reason, for only eating bread once a day, the explanation turns to more abstract justifications. Perhaps it becomes 'bad luck' to eat bread after midday. Perhaps it becomes 'good luck' to start the day with toast.

Superstitions tend to come from a place of reason. At least, it was reasoned at some point in time. The ones we still follow today were once strongly held beliefs, perhaps from religious practices, or from practicalities of daily life.

It's believed that the idea that it's bad luck to open an umbrella indoors came from the fact that Victorian umbrellas were clumsy, with unreliable opening mechanisms. By opening one indoors, you were simply risking an accident.

Walking under ladders being bad luck originates from ancient Egypt, where it was thought that passing through the triangle created by a leaning ladder was an offence to the trinity of Gods. The number three has held significance in many religions, and Christian culture adopted this superstition with their own teachings of the holy trinity.

However pointless or abstract a superstition might seem to a modern society, they actually come from places of reason and practicality. They just become irrelevant as life changes and moves on. But, of course, that doesn't mean they become less prevalent, or that they have no impact on the lives of your characters. People are still incredibly superstitious, particularly in certain circles.

Superstitions around boats and sailing are abundant, springing from the fact that it is an incredibly dangerous occupation. Water is unpredictable and a huge unknown, even today. It has been personified by countless cultures: worshipped and feared in equal measure. The theatre also has its own vast collection of superstitions, with many of them springing from a need to stay safe. It's an environment in which huge, heavy pieces of scenery are being moved around, and these superstitions have sprung from necessities. Although, some superstitions exist just to promote a particular actor, and push them forward into 'the limelight'!

It may be that, long ago, wolves roamed the nearby woods. It might have led to practices of locking and blacking out windows at night, regardless of the heat. It might have led to practices of not cooking after sunset, and never disposing of meat bones until the following morning. These may have become superstitions, still practised long after the trees were felled and the wolves moved on.

Maybe your culture's religion once practised polygamy. Even though the tradition was abandoned generations ago, even if the religion is no longer followed at all, it might remain as a superstition that having only one wife is bad luck. Perhaps people have double wedding ceremonies, essentially marrying the same partner twice, in order to trick the Gods, and receive their blessing for the partnership.

Have a think about superstitions that remain in your culture, even if their reasoning is long passed, or even, long forgotten. Consider the origins of those beliefs, and how the remaining importance of them might impact your characters and their journeys.

SUPERSTITIONS AND THEIR ORIGINS:

BAD MANNERS AND INSULTS

In some cultures, it's seen as an insult to tip a worker. In some, giving someone a thumbs up is akin to giving them the middle finger. In others, having one hand in your pocket, or eating in the street, or finishing all of your meal is considered bad manners.

What is rude in your fictional world? What would cause insult or upset?

Whatever acts you choose to be social faux pas, they are not considered as rude for no reason. They are created within the culture, as a product of the world and its history.

Things that are rude, just like your superstitions, might spring from practicalities of everyday life. Perhaps, after years of droughts, floods, and deadly storms, discussing the weather became rude. Perhaps simply saying 'lovely day' to your neighbour is an insulting faux pas because it's tempting fate. A fate that has dealt your world some harsh blows.

Maybe your country is an island, with half of the population employed in marine-based occupations. Suffering from sea-sickness might be viewed as an insult to the ship's captain. It might be a terrible insult to have an outdoor light on your house, for fear it might be mistaken for a lighthouse. It might be the height of rudeness to refuse a fish course from your host.

Other bad manners might spring from your world's religion. It might be rude to shake hands with your religious leaders, especially if you're a manual worker with rough skin on your palms. It might be rude to take your shoes off before retiring to bed, or to wear long hair loose in public, or to cross a threshold while still wearing your hat.

Bad manners can also be politically motivated, such as it being impolite to discuss income, money matters, or talk about investments. It might be impolite to speak another language in public, or to fail to salute a member of the council, or to have doors that are hinged to be opened by the left hand.

You might have bad manners in your world that are related to magic, or to space travel, or to AI, robots, time travel, or dragons. Perhaps it's rude to land a space ship to the left hand side of another, because of the way the boosters are aligned. Maybe it's rude to roll your sleeves up in a magic academy because you're implying your fellow magicians are mere tricksters with items tucked up under their cuffs. It might be impolite to feed another person's dragon, or to wear any gold. Maybe it's insulting to give your robot a human name, or to assign a gender to them.

You can also have fun creating unique insults and curse words for your world, always being certain to embed them into the world's history and culture.

In your world with extreme weather, calling someone a 'sky gazer' might be akin to calling them a brainless idiot, suggesting that they simply gawp at the incoming storm rather than preparing for its arrival. In your island community, calling someone a 'rock clinger' might mean that they're a coward, and too scared to step off the rock of the island.

Again, these insults can come from general practicalities, and the way your world works day-by-day. They can be based in religion, or politics, or they can come from prejudice regarding people of different demographics.

They can be used to great effect when creating conflict for your characters, or building up tension in your communities. Especially when different cultures cross borders, and social faux pas are unknown and misunderstood.

RUDE BEHAVIOURS AND THEIR ORIGINS:
COMMON INSULTS AND THEIR ORIGINS:

HEROES AND VILLAINS

For every hero, there is also a villain. For every heroic act, there is a villainous one. For every exulted personality trait, there is a condemned one. And for every scapegoat, there is someone being protected, their wrongdoings concealed.

While your story has its protagonists and its antagonists, so too does your culture.

First up, your culture will have historic heroes. Maybe your society sees its founders as heroes. The first government, or the first warriors. Perhaps it has a patron saint who killed a monster, or burnt witches, or protected magic for future generations. It may well have myths and legends telling of great heroes, that may or may not have actually existed. Maybe they killed the Gods, or made the land fertile, or brought women to a community made solely of men.

And while there are stories of historic heroes, they will also have their villains.

People who diverted a stream, cutting off a community. Someone that stole children, caused a famine, or cursed a country. Perhaps the founders are seen as villains, perhaps the society was built on the back of slavery, or child labour, or people trafficking.

And always remember that there are also people who seek to do something heroic, but end up, unintentionally, doing something villainous instead. Introducing a foreign plant species that wipes out crops, eradicating a predator that is much-needed in the eco-system.

In addition, there are also heroes that, as more information comes to light, or as society's attitudes change over the years, lose their hero status. And there are those who might transition from villain to hero. And there are those that are heroes, but their one villainous act is so evil, so cruel, that it outweighs all the good that they also did. As like every aspect of your world, heroics are not black and white.

Let's skip to the present, and think about the kind of people that are seen as heroes or villains. Because this tells a lot about your culture: who is placed on a pedestal, and who is kicked to the gutter.

It might be that sporting achievements raise someone to heroic status. Perhaps military honours. Maybe emergency workers, healers, magicians, or farmers are seen as heroes. Perhaps it's those who raise money for charity, or who dedicate their time to helping others. Maybe it's entertainers, and people who make the world fun, or help people forget their problems.

The qualities that these people possess—the traits, skills, and personalities—become the traits that people strive to have themselves. The physical strength, the kindness, the talents and skills. It's what makes a child stand up in class and say "When I grow up, I want to be..." But, as these particular traits become the desired ones, other traits become undesirable. And certain people are left on the sidelines, with no hope of ever becoming a hero.

There may be very specific circumstances or events that create new heroes. Perhaps farmers for working twice as hard to feed the population during a famine, or miners who dig out survivors after a landslip or earthquake. Maybe an infertility doctor, or someone who creates a vaccine, or the inventor of new technology. It might be police officers during a crime wave, or religious leaders who ended a drought (or so they say), or a teacher who introduced a new way of thinking about the world.

And then you have the controversial heroes. Those who are heroes to some, and villains to others. The rebels, the revolutionaries, the protestors. Those seeking to topple the status quo. Those looking to protect freedom of speech and expression. Those who want to change the norms and expectations, who want to shift culture forwards, or sideways, or turn it upside-down altogether.

So, let's think about propaganda, scapegoats, and lies. There have always been groups of people vilified to fit a narrative. Often propelled by political (including economic) or religious motives. They may have done nothing more than simply exist.

Think about *why* these people become scapegoats. Think about *why* they're portrayed as villains. They go against a narrative. They might be a figure that promotes freedom, vilified by an authoritarian government. They might be a figure that promotes equality, vilified by greedy capitalists. They might be a figure that promotes modern ideals of morality, vilified by a strict religion.

People might not, yet, understand their motives. They might not, yet, realise that this person could, in fact, be the hero they desperately need. They might be so indoctrinated in their culture that the idea of change is far too terrifying, too radical for them to accept. People can be convinced to vote against what's good for them. And people do push against change. The known is far more comfortable than the unknown, even if the known is not that great.

Whole demographics of your society can become vilified. They can be dehumanised, so that the wider population don't see them as equal, and don't care about their hardships. The poor, the working class, immigrants, the uneducated, women, those with magical powers. If people believe that such demographics are inherently bad, that they are responsible for their own hardships, and even responsible for all the hardships in society, the status quo can be maintained. Oppression and inequality can continue, and no one will care.

No one, that is, until a true hero rises up...

HISTORICAL HEROES:
HISTORICAL VILLAINS:
CONTEMPORARY HEROES:
CONTEMPORARY VILLAINS:
SCAPEGOATS:

SUBCULTURES AND ALTERNATIVE LIFESTYLES

Existing within any culture, there are subcultures. Sometimes, these subcultures include a vast number of people, and large percentages of the population. It might be a subculture distinguished by religion, or by ethnicity. Alternatively, there are niche subcultures, distinguished by things such as music tastes or dietary choices.

A subculture isn't necessarily a rebellion against the main norms and expectations of society. Indeed, subcultures often live quite happily within the main culture. People can also be members of different subcultures simultaneously. They're basically creating a world of their own, within the wider world.

A subculture might emerge through choice. A seeking of solidarity, of finding one's tribe. Just like-minded souls coming together. Alternatively, subcultures might arise through a need for security and safety. An oppressed group may come together to seek solace and protection. They may feel ostracised, or pushed out of the main culture, leaving them little choice but to create a safe space of their own.

Some subcultures will arise from direct opposition to popular and mainstream culture (these are often termed as countercultures), as there may be aspects they disagree with, or things that they feel the need to actively fight against. Subcultures might arise from a refusal to integrate with a foreign culture, a need to keep hold of cultural roots, or a desire to hold onto older, traditional values in a culture that is modernising itself.

Some of the subcultures in your world might be protected by laws. They might have rights and allowances, such as religious practices or traditional activities. Perhaps they are allowed extra holidays, or allowances must be made for them in the workplace. Maybe they have rights to wear particular clothing, or forego safety laws. They might be allowed to carry ceremonial weapons, or have access to otherwise banned books.

There may also be laws to protect these groups from discrimination, oppression, or violence.

And then, there may be subcultures that are made illegal. Perhaps migrants are legally required to integrate, fully, with the culture they come into. They might be banned from speaking their own language, or practising their own religions, or celebrating their own calendars. They might be viewed as being too subversive, too dangerous, or too much of a threat to those in power.

Lesser than a subculture, or perhaps precursors to them, are alternative lifestyles. Choices and decisions that are seen as being outside of the norms and expectations that you've already established.

It might be unusual living arrangements, treatment of the environment or animals. Perhaps the way people educate their children, the way they parent, or their political stance. Maybe it's an unusual religious or dietary choice. While the choices made are recognisably outside of the norm, it may not be widespread or defined enough to be generally accepted as an actual subculture. But as a demographic grows, they might seek to be recognised, they might unite for extra rights or protections.

Think about how subcultures are viewed by your society. Perhaps they are accepted, and their diverse natures celebrated. Maybe they are disliked, and considered to be subversive, even if they're actually quite harmless.

SUBCULTURES THAT EXIST ALONGSIDE THE MAIN CULTURE:
SUBCULTURES THAT OPPOSE THE MAIN CULTURE:
SUBCULTURES PROTECTED BY LAW:
CRIMINALISED SUBCULTURES:
ALTERNATIVE LIFESTYLE CHOICES:

FAMILY STRUCTURES

Who sits at the head of the family? Is it the one bringing in the most money? The person who runs the domestic space? Perhaps it's the oldest family member, or the most educated, or the strongest. Maybe the youngest generation makes all the decisions, bringing a fresh perspective to family life.

Family structures might reflect the hierarchy of the wider culture: a patriarchal family structure in a patriarchal society. Or, it might subvert it: placing a matriarch at the head of the family instead.

Naturally, families will differ. They might have a different head to the norm because of illness or death. It might be that the natural head of the family has little interest in the role. Maybe someone else is simply more capable. But, there will be norms and expectations for families. There will be those that follow the typical structure, and those that subvert it.

How important is family in your world? It might be the centre of everything, with cultural values based around good, traditional family values. Perhaps family time is sacred, and the school and working days are arranged in a way to allow for maximum family time. Alternatively, it might be that family is little more than a birth situation. Found family might be more important than biological family. Perhaps children leave home at a young age, perhaps for education or to take up an apprenticeship. Maybe a parent's job is done by the time their child is six years old.

Children might be raised collectively, breastfeeding from whichever woman is available, seeking comfort from whichever arms are closest. Perhaps women don't even keep track of which particular children are biologically theirs (although, you'll have to consider the implications of this on the collective gene pool).

How many generations of the family live together? Perhaps the norm is to see four generations in the same house. Or maybe they live separately, but close by. Maybe in neighbouring houses, or always staying in the same towns and areas. This set-up would require consideration of how easy it is to find work and housing close to where people grew up. Maybe children are never raised by their parents. Maybe grandparents raise their grandchildren, freeing the parents up to pursue their careers.

And what about the wider family? Aunts, uncles, cousins? Does everyone live close to one another, or do they spread wider apart?

How is family tracked? How do they know who's related to who? Regardless of the typical family structures in your world, biological relations need to be tracked to avoid incest. For the health of your society, it's important to keep the gene pool deep. Perhaps an elderly matriarch carries the family tree in her head. Maybe families keep detailed records, or maybe records are kept centrally by the authorities.

Do couples get married? Perhaps there is a different commitment contract or ceremony that seals their partnership. And how is that partnership shown? Does one person move out of their own home to live in their partner's house? Do couples change their names to match, or wear rings? Perhaps partnerships are marked with tattoos, or piercings, or the families pooling their assets.

It might be that one partner becomes the legal property of the other, or a whole family become the property of the other family. Maybe, when partnerships are formed, the couple leave behind all of their possessions, and start afresh, together. Maybe they leave behind their family ties, moving on in life entirely. Becoming, essentially, a new person.

The set-up of the family, the importance and closeness of it, will have a big impact on your characters. Families are the first places we learn morals and values, roles and norms. Families might be responsible for education and socialisation. They might be responsible for religious instruction. They might be responsible for work experience, for future careers, or for choosing future partners.

HEAD OF THE FAMILY:
THE IMPORTANCE OF FAMILY:
HOW DIFFERENT GENERATIONS LIVE TOGETHER:
HOW FAMILY TREES ARE TRACKED:
MARRIAGE AND PARTNERSHIPS:

PREGNANCY, BIRTH, AND MOTHERHOOD

Just because women are the ones experiencing pregnancy and giving birth (assuming you're not creating characters of a species in which this isn't the case), doesn't mean that women get to control the situation. In fact, they might have very few choices at all.

Perhaps pregnancy and birth is solely the woman's domain. Maybe they are separated from men early on in their pregnancy, retreating to a place where only women are allowed. Perhaps men aren't allowed to be present at the birth of their own children. Perhaps the entire process is something quite mystical and unknown to them.

Or, it might be that pregnancy is more of a shared experience. Perhaps the father supports the mother through every step, delivering the child himself, and taking his equal share of sleepless nights. Perhaps a pregnancy is shared by the entire community, with women giving birth surrounded by their whole village.

Maybe your culture is based on surrogacy, with younger women passing their children over to the older women to be raised. Maybe the only role of the biological mothers is to breastfeed, while their children benefit from the wisdom of more experienced women.

It might be that, in your fictional world, women are required to give birth. It might be viewed, culturally, as their duty and responsibility, or their role and purpose. Or it might be legislated by law. Perhaps your society is desperately trying to replenish its population. Or, births might be restricted to try and control a growing population.

How are pregnant women viewed in your world's culture? Are they celebrated and glorified? Are they thought of as beautiful, fruitful, exulted? Perhaps they're removed from view, hidden away until after the birth. Maybe it's because your culture views pregnancy as shameful, or as a weakened state. Perhaps as highly private, or maybe boastful. Maybe your world's religion teaches that pregnant women are more susceptible to corruption by evil forces, and expects them to withdraw for months of prayer.

It may well be that some pregnant women are thought of as virtuous, while others are vilified. Perhaps people will congratulate a wealthy woman on her pregnancy, but judge a poor woman as reckless. Maybe older women are praised for pregnancies, while young women are criticised. Perhaps it's the other way around.

The values your culture has around marriage, family, stability, wealth, and the role of women will impact this. Which women are 'good' candidates for becoming mothers? Which are 'bad'?

The way your culture views pregnant women may well impact the kind of healthcare available to them. A culture that finds them beautiful might have far better maternity care available than a culture that views pregnancy as shameful.

What healthcare provisions are available, and how much choice do women have? Are they forced into sterile hospital environments? Do they receive pain relief whether they want it or not? Perhaps their only choice is a home birth with whoever is available to help.

And how expensive is healthcare? There might be a huge difference between the healthcare available to rich and poor, or to those living in cities versus those in rural areas. But remember that modernised, clinical healthcare isn't always better. It might be that, in your world, the village wise women have a far lower record of infant mortality than the expensive city doctors. Maybe those wise women have secrets they are unwilling to share.

And what about after the birth? What about the first few months of new parenthood? Is the mother assisted by the other women in her community? It might be the norm for women to receive full-time support from their own mother, or from their mother-in-law. Perhaps younger, unmarried women are recruited (whether paid or unpaid) to help out. Maybe it's seen as shameful and an admittance of inadequacy for a woman to enlist any help.

Maybe the mother and father take on entirely equal roles. Maybe the father takes on the heavy lifting while the mother recovers from the birth.

You'll need to think, also, about the logistics and the finances. Do people get paid maternity and paternity leave from work? Is a woman expected to give up her job once she becomes a mother? Perhaps the new parents give up their own home and move in with the grandparents. Maybe they move into a community building with plenty of help on hand.

It might be that, only upon the birth of their first child, that their marriage is legitimised. In which case, you'd have to think about how infertility is handled in the culture. Maybe any role the parents had before is given up, and they become nothing more than full-time parents to their child.

Remember to consider whether this is the same for all parents, or whether there are differences based on personal circumstances or characteristics.

Are children seen as a burden? A blessing? Can life carry on, relatively, normally, or is everything turned on its head?

WHO SUPPORTS THE MOTHER THROUGH PREGNANCY?

WHO IS PRESENT AT THE BIRTH?
HOW ARE PREGNANT WOMEN VIEWED?
MATERNITY HEALTHCARE AVAILABLE:
DISCREPANCIES IN HEALTHCARE:

WHO HELPS AFTER THE BIRTH?
HOW DOES LIFE CHANGE FOR THE PARENTS?

COMING OF AGE

There are many potential coming of age moments for the young people in your world. While some may be celebrated and greatly anticipated, some might be feared, by parents and children alike.

Growing up can be difficult and scary, but it's also something that many young people are keen to do, often before their parents believe they're ready. Coming of age markers, celebrations, and milestones are a way to both celebrate a growing person, but also to control and pace that growth.

It is quite common for girls and boys to have different milestones, as they mature differently both physically and emotionally.

Consider when a character might officially become an adult. Is it at age 18? 21 years old? Maybe it's at 15 or even 12 that they shrug off childhood for adult responsibilities. It might not be a set age, but based on educational achievement, or a physical strength test. It might be the loss of their last baby tooth, or their first period.

Some coming of age milestones are physical ones, over which we have no control. A girl can't choose when she has her first period, just as a boy can't choose when his voice breaks. Others are set markers, maybe set down in law, such as age of consent, legal driving and drinking age, or the age at which they can vote.

Coming of age milestones will be impacted by other aspects of your culture, such as gender roles, education, and family set-up. In a patriarchal culture, boys might be expected to take on adult roles before girls. In a culture with a low population (perhaps after years of war, or famine, or a widespread natural disaster), laws might be changed to allow girls to marry and have children younger than before. If your education system keeps children in compulsory schooling until age 18, they are unlikely to be viewed as fully-fledged adults before that age. In a society where work is valued above education, children may move onto apprenticeships and paid employment just as they hit their teens.

Perhaps periods are celebrated in your culture. Maybe there is no shame surrounding them, and a girl's first bloodied bedsheets are hung outside her house on display. Perhaps, each year, girls who have started their periods are dressed up on May Day, and paraded through the streets to applause and cheering. But what happens to girls who develop later? Or those who don't have periods at all? Maybe girls fake their own periods, for fear of shaming their parents. For fear of being trapped in a perpetual state of childhood. How, in turn, does this impact the way children are viewed in your wider culture? How does it impact how women are viewed; their roles, their responsibilities? How does it impact the age at which girls become sexualised?

It might be that, in order to transition into manhood, a boy is expected to pass a physical test. Maybe he has to fight a grown man, perhaps he has to kill a wolf, or build his own house. But what happens to the boys who are physically unable? The weaker boys, the shorter boys, the less fit boys? What about the boys with disabilities? This will be impacted by the body standards in your culture. If physical strength is valued above all, a weak boy is unlikely to receive any help in his endeavours to become a man. But in a culture that promotes kindness, support, and raising one another up, the community may well rally round to help those who are less able.

While there may be many coming of age milestones that a child is eager and impatient to reach, there may be others that are deeply feared. Perhaps just by the children themselves, with their parents pushing them on, encouraging them, comforting them that it won't be as bad as they imagine, or even shaming them for their hesitancy. Or those feared by parents and children alike. What lengths might parents go to to protect their children from what awaits? Faking the milestone? Moving away? Never registering their children's births?

A transition from childhood to adulthood can be brutal, violent even. It can be a test of strength, of will, of resilience. However cruel, the adults in your culture might wholeheartedly believe that it is the best way to prepare their children for adulthood. Perhaps children are expected to lose their virginity publicly. Maybe it's required that this transition into adulthood is observed and verified. Perhaps they can't choose their partner. Perhaps they can't choose when it happens. Maybe children are scarred, cut, tattooed, or even mutilated to mark their move into adulthood.

Alternatively, your world's culture might value childhood above adulthood, encouraging children to maintain their innocence for as long as possible. Maybe they're protected and pampered. Maybe their transition is made as easy as possible, with allowances made for hormonal mood swings and the confusion of puberty. Maybe girls hide their periods, maybe their mothers help to cover them up, desperately conserving their childhood. Perhaps baby teeth that are lost are mourned, perhaps they are ritualistically buried, or preserved, or hidden away.

As children move into adulthood, the responsibilities placed on them increase, and the expectations increase along with them. Looking back to the norms and values that you laid out for your culture, what might specifically be expected of those moving from childhood to adulthood?

When are they expected to leave home? It might be at a specific age, or it might be at a more flexible milestone such as gaining their first job, getting married, or not until they are deemed financially stable or responsible enough.

What else is expected of them? Maybe they are expected to financially compensate their parents for raising them (now there's an idea!), or to take care of their parents physically. Maybe they are expected to take on the care of their younger siblings, or to take over the family business. It might be that they're expected to move away from their parents, cutting off contact, and that this is believed to be the best way to establish their independence. But what happens when the expectations are too much? What happens to the children that fail in the eyes of their culture?

WHEN DOES A CHILD OFFICIALLY BECOME AN ADULT?
CELEBRATED COMING OF AGE MILESTONES:
UNACKNOWLEDGED COMING OF AGE MILESTONES:
HOW THE TRANSITION INTO ADULTHOOD IS MARKED:
LAWS REGARDING COMING OF AGE:
WHEN ARE CHILDREN EXPECTED TO LEAVE HOME?
EXPECTATIONS PLACED ON THOSE ENTERING ADULTHOOD:

RITES OF PASSAGE

There are many milestones within a lifetime, and many of them have their own rituals and ceremonies. Their own celebrations and festivals. Every year, we mark the passing of time with a birthday, which has its own set of rituals. Presents, cakes, cards, songs. Even before we are born, there might be rituals around the first scan, or revealing the gender or name.

Since the rise of social media in our lives, it often feels like these rites of passage have become even more numerous, although it might simply be that they're more visible. Everything from photos marking the first day of each new school year, to posting photos of first house keys, our lives are filled with markers and memories of these life milestones.

Before you dive into creating rites of passage in your world, I want you to think for a moment *why* we mark these moments. Some mark the passage of time, some mark personal achievements. There are some that are tied up in legalities, such as the first legal drink on your 18th birthday (in the UK, at least), and the obsolete significance of the 21st birthday, which is still celebrated here as something special, but no longer holds any legal importance. There are birth registrations, marriages, and divorces. There are also religious milestones such as confirmations and coming of age ceremonies. Moments when someone's religious devotion moves up a step. And then there are cultural rites of passage, when you achieve all those norms and expectations set out by your culture: first house, first job, first child. First son.

Beyond the widespread rites of passage, there are always more personal and private ones. There may be celebrations that are carried out within the family home, but not shared publicly. First period, sobriety milestones, when a criminal conviction is no longer held on record. Perhaps the publication of a book. Because everyone has milestones that are personal to their own journey in life, outside of those deemed as the norm by society.

Your world may also have magical rites of passage, or different milestones for the different species of your world. Characters expected to live for thousands of years may not bother celebrating every single birthday!

Let's pull it back to the cultural norms and expectations you've laid out for your characters. What is important in your world's culture? What moments, what achievements are considered ones for celebration? Which milestones would people brag about, or share publicly? Which milestones are outside of the norm, or more private?

And remember that not all rites of passage are a time for celebration. The most obvious are rituals surrounding death. Beyond the personal loss of those who are bereaved, your wider society might lose a significant or beloved figure. Your society might be losing someone they truly needed: a leader, a revolutionist, a warrior, a healer. They might be losing their very last mage, or traditional skills, or knowledge. And still, beyond all of that, everyone is reminded that they are mortal. They are faced with the one truth society attempts to run from: that everyone dies.

While your characters might celebrate a life lived, or the transition of a soul to some other realm or existence (or perhaps they believe the soul will stay there with them), it will still stand as a reminder of mortality. The death rituals might be sanitised, or hidden away. People may prefer to ignore it all. Maybe the deceased person is dressed up, preserved, made to look alive.

Your world may also have rituals that are trials, or an endurance. There might be rituals that are painful, involve surgery or tattoos, or that involve mutilation of the body. Not every stage in life is a good one, or a pleasant one.

And consider rites of passage that are no longer practised. Ones that have become outdated, ones that no longer follow the values of society, ones that have been outlawed. As your culture develops, rites of passage will shift, change, lose or gain significance and meaning. Rituals from migrating cultures might be adopted, or incorporated into other rituals, while others might be lost to time altogether.

RITES OF PASSAGE CELEBRATIONS FOR:

BIRTHS:
BIRTHDAYS:
EDUCATIONAL MILESTONES:

RELIGIOUS MILESTONES:
OTHER LIFE MILESTONES:
MARRIAGES:
DEATHS:
HOW RITES OF PASSAGE HAVE CHANGED:

LOVE AND ROMANCE

Romantic love doesn't exist in every culture. There are many theories and beliefs about love, from the pragmatic idea that it's nothing more than a chemical charge prompting us to procreate, to the charming notion that love is what makes the world go round.

Love has moved humans to write poetry (however badly), write music, paint, create, and build impressive structures and monuments. It's also moved humans to do crazy things, to cry, to despair, even to kill. Love has prompted people to do things they never believed themselves possible of.

Love has also guaranteed the continuation of the species. From the desire to breed, to the drive to protect offspring no matter what. Love, whatever it actually is, plays a big part in ensuring the future of the human race. So perhaps, as far as we're concerned, it really does make the world go round.

Have a think about the culture you've created so far. Does it seem like the place where people would be romantic and idealistic? If your culture is very pragmatic and logic, they may be less inclined to romanticise love. On the other hand, it might provide welcome relief from the practicalities of daily life. Your culture might glorify and revere romantic love, perhaps it's a driving force, held above everything else.

Maybe love is viewed as a weakness, depriving people of sense. Maybe love is viewed as a curse or bewitchment. It might be that mages are blamed for love, that they purposefully use it to distract people from what's really going on. Perhaps the idea of love has become outdated, or impractical, or maybe science has irrefutably disproven its existence.

Are people free to partner and marry for love? Or are there more important motivations? It might be more important to choose partners for money, or property, profession, or for their genetics. It might be that some people are freer to choose their partners than others are. Perhaps girls have more choice, or working class people.

What acts are considered to be romantic? Is it all flowers and chocolates, or something else? Maybe romance is kindness, or coyness. Maybe it's complimenting your partner on their educational achievements, or their cooking skills. Perhaps it's showing off your own strength, fighting skills, or debate skills. How do people in your world attract a partner and, subsequently, woo them?

It might be that all romantic relationships begin as friendships, or maybe romance comes after the wedding.

And consider how romance changes through the relationship. It might begin with candlelit dinners but, over time, it might become foot rubs and making coffee without being asked.

Does your culture have celebrations of love, such as Valentine's Day? Do they celebrate anniversaries? And how are these events celebrated?

And think about the make up of a relationship. Are they monogamous, with each person taking only one partner at a time? Perhaps they're polygamous, and free to marry more than one person, or polyamorous, and practising open relationships. Polygyny (one man, many women) and polyandry (one woman, many men) are also options. Perhaps, in your world, there's a completely unique set up for relationships.

DOES YOUR CULTURE BELIEVE IN ROMANTIC LOVE?
CAN PEOPLE PARTNER FOR LOVE?
TYPICAL ACTS OF ROMANCE:
ROMANTIC CELEBRATIONS:
PARTNERSHIP STRUCTURES (monogamy, etc):

SEXUALITY

How sexy is your culture? I'm joking, of course. Well… sort of. How is sexuality viewed? Is it private and secret? Perhaps your characters are demure, and always dress modestly. Maybe they parade down the street in barely any clothes at all. Perhaps everyone is always naked (but, please, give them a warm climate!)

There may well be laws surrounding sexuality; such as a legal age of consent, or rules about who can have sex with who, and in what circumstances. There may be laws to protect against abuse, assault, and rape. There may be laws around public decency.

Remember that ideas around sexuality are likely to differ by generation. As society evolves and adapts over time, and as each new generation rebels and rejects the moral codes that came before, seeking their own version of morality, so attitudes shift. And it might happen slowly and gently, with everyone easing into the new ways, and gracefully pushing their prudery aside. It might, however, happen suddenly, as an act of rebellion, leaving people shocked and disgusted. Rules and laws may quickly be reeled in tighter, fighting against the new liberalism.

And just as these differences, these micro-cultures, will exist across the different ages, they will also exist across other demographics too.

Perhaps people are more relaxed about sexuality in the modern cities, while those in the country cling to older codes of morality. Maybe girls are held to different standards than boys, or adults are expected to cast their sexual freedoms aside and act more 'responsibly'.

There are likely to be different codes of behaviour in certain institutions, such as religions, educational settings, and private member clubs.

Consider where sexuality is evident in your world, and what contradictions that might involve. Perhaps brothels are as common as corner shops, and red light districts exist alongside shopping centres, even though citizens are expected to live to a strict moral code, dressing in clothes that cover them from the neck to the ankle. Maybe sexuality is only a playground for the rich, with exclusive and expensive sex clubs, while average citizens are expected to keep every hint of sexuality tightly locked behind their bedroom doors.

In the great sexual revolution, who has been left behind or excluded? Who has refused to join in?

It may be that codes of conduct have become stricter, either through legal enforcement, or through a rebellion against the looser morals of the older generation. Perhaps young people have decided to be more private about it, or chosen to reject it altogether. Perhaps, in a dystopian future where women are seen as little more than baby-making factories, young women are choosing to take control of their sexuality through abstinence. Or perhaps a new religion sweeps in, catching the attention of young people, and convincing them to follow its strict moral code.

Perhaps sexuality is hijacked by need: a dramatic fall in population, widespread infertility, or a rise in infant mortality. Maybe attitudes need to change quickly, in order to protect the future of your world.

SEXUALITY LAWS:
DIFFERING VIEWS OF SEXUALITY:
HOW PUBLIC IS SEXUALITY?
WHAT CONTRADICTIONS EXIST?

GENDER AND GENDER ROLES

Which genders are recognised in your society? Which are not recognised? Perhaps they have more than we could name, perhaps they have none at all.

It's important to understand the difference between sex and gender. These words are, far too often, used interchangeably. Sex is biological (although it's far more complicated than we tend to understand), and gender is a cultural and social construct. At birth, our sex is assigned by our external sexual organs (which doesn't always match the internal organs, chromosomes, hormones, or other biological identifiers). We tend, culturally, to accept that the assigned sex is the same as the gender.

But maybe, in your world, gender isn't assigned at birth, but assigned in early childhood based on their characteristics and personality. Perhaps it is left unassigned until adolescence or the end of puberty. Maybe people choose for themselves.

Consider how records of births are kept. Whether it's simply remembered by the head of each family or a village elder, or formally registered and kept centrally for the entire country, records of birth are important simply to keep an eye on the gene pool and reduce inbreeding. But does gender get recorded? Does it even matter?

Does your culture recognise gender identity as being separate to biological sex, or is it seen as being the same thing? Perhaps they view it as entirely unrelated. Perhaps one holds precedence over the other. Perhaps neither are taken into any consideration.

Why would someone's biological sex or gender identity matter in a society? Generally, humans like order. They like patterns and segments and a way of categorising the world to make sense of it. From birth, we start looking for patterns. When a baby cries, it's picked up. It's fed, or cuddled, or changed. Its needs are met. That's a pattern. But why does gender matter?

In our culture, gender is used to provide a division of roles, of behaviours, of expectations. The behaviours, likes, dislikes, traits, and aspirations associated with any gender is entirely a social construct. From the moment of our birth, and the assignment of our sex, those expectations are placed upon us and reinforced by the toys we're given, the way people act around and towards us, the way we're educated, and the roles we're expected to take as adults. Whether fairly or unfairly, these gender expectations are imprinted on us, generation after generation.

Of course, as culture changes, so too do these expectations. For centuries, babies of any gender wore white dresses through early childhood. It was practical, with all the dirt easily bleached out. Gender-specific clothing didn't really arrive until the First World War, with pink chosen for boys and blue for girls. It wasn't until around the 1940s that the colours switched to what we recognise today. Gender-specific clothing is a very new construct.

Likewise, the idea of women being naturally caring and nurturing didn't take root until the rise of the housewife in Western culture. Before that, wealthy mothers barely saw their children, who were cared for by nannies and governesses, and the mothers of the industrial revolution worked long, gruelling hours, with no time to spend with their children. The 'natural order' as we see it today, is a product of changing culture, which is a product of changing roles for women based on society's need.

I'm risking turning this into a history lesson now, but it's important to understand how gender roles are culturally assigned, because the culture you're creating may have an entirely different way of handling gender.

What typical roles are assigned for the different genders in your world? And what are those roles based on? What does society need from its different citizens? Changes will come about through things such as technological advances, migration, political shifts, revolution, big events such as war, natural disasters, pandemics, etc. And the expected roles will change along with them. People might be required to take on jobs that were previously unusual for their gender. They might be required, in turn, to give up those jobs and return to their former roles.

How are the roles and expectations enforced? Is it through public shame, or through laws? There may be laws that prevent certain genders from doing certain things, such as using public swimming pools, or wearing certain clothes, or leaving the house when they're menstruating. What are the repercussions of breaking out of expected gender roles?

Of course, we can't side-step biological sex altogether. When it comes to reproduction, there is only a certain portion of the population who are able to become pregnant, and to breastfeed. And due to a wide number of different factors, this is not sex-specific in every case. There are many people unable to produce offspring for all kinds of reasons. And that's before you even bring in the option of personal choice or circumstance.

Those who can bear children are, however progressive or equal your society is, locked into that role. Unless, of course, you're talking about non-human characters or a society with technology that invalidates this. But, largely, there will be people who can become pregnant, and people who can't. This produces a need in your culture. A need for healthcare, a need for adaptations and exceptions. It produces, almost certainly, an unlevel playing field. At least, for a portion of someone's life. There's also menstruation and menopause to consider as other potential interruptions.

And your world may have other biological differences. Maybe only one gender can perform magic. Maybe it's a certain part of their body, or a hormone that increases magical power. Maybe your society figures out a way to synthetically reproduce it.

Perhaps your culture has found a way to level it back out. Perhaps it's swung one way or another. Perhaps it simply doesn't care about making things even.

RECOGNISED GENDERS:
HOW IS GENDER ASSIGNED?
IS IT THE SAME AS BIOLOGICAL SEX?
TYPICAL GENDER ROLES AND EXPECTATIONS:
THE STANCE ON EQUALITY:
LAWS SURROUNDING GENDER:

HEALTH, FITNESS, AND BEAUTY STANDARDS

What does it mean to be 'healthy' in your world? Physical strength? Sporting prowess? Perhaps mental health and emotional health are valued equally to physical health. Perhaps they are viewed as being inseparable.

What do people in your world do to become healthier? Perhaps they eat less and exercise more. Perhaps they eat more and bulk up their muscle. Maybe they meditate, practice yoga, or talk out their feelings. Maybe they take long walks and stare at the scenery.

If the main industry of your country requires high numbers of manual workers, such as farming, mining, fishing, or forestry, then strength and physical fitness may be seen as the ideal. Although the rich may shun it, in order to differentiate themselves. Perhaps your country, however, thrives on an industry of cottage crafts. Of delicate lace-making or weaving. Perhaps dexterity and a sharp mind are valued over strength. Perhaps long, slender fingers are sought after. Maybe your magic system is based on dance, and the peak of fitness is measured in balance and flexibility.

How do people view sickness and disability? Are people hidden away from view? Are their disabilities and illnesses viewed as weaknesses? As flaws? Perhaps, even, as punishments. Maybe they are pitied, maybe they become charity cases. Perhaps they are vilified, or maybe they're valued for their other strengths and abilities. Maybe they're believed to be closer to God, or to be marked as special, or to be the next step in human evolution.

Perhaps the way they're viewed changes suddenly when a disabled monarch is crowned, or when the leader of the country falls ill.

Also, consider whether physical disabilities and symptoms are viewed differently to mental disabilities and health problems. Maybe they are treated together, maybe separately. Maybe there is no effort made to ease, cure, or make adjustments for them.

What is the ideal body in your world, and how is it achieved and maintained? Is it different for men and women? Is it different for older and younger people? Perhaps there is no beauty standard to strive for at all.

Throughout history, beauty standards have shifted and changed. Once upon a time, a tan was undesirable, as it denoted labouring outside. It meant that someone was poor. Likewise, slim figures were seen as a result of not having enough to eat.

Also, throughout history, and across the world, people have suffered for beauty standards. From boned corsets that broke ribs and damaged internal organs, and make-up filled with poisons and toxins, all the way to extreme body modification. And what is beautiful in one culture, can seem like mutilation or torture to another.

Body modification is common the world over, and it's not a modern invention, either. From piercings and tattoos to elongated body parts and cosmetic surgery. How far do the body modifications go in the culture you're creating? What is seen as beautiful, and why? Where did the traditions come from? And when did they stop?

Certain beauty ideals may fall out of fashion over time. They might be revealed as being unhealthy, or deadly. They might fall behind technology. They might be forced to end due to war, lack of supply, famine. They may even become illegal.

Consider whether everyone is held to the same beauty ideals, or if standards are different across different demographics. Perhaps women have higher standards to strive for, or young men. Maybe more is expected of the rich, or the magical, or the different species that exist in your world.

And think about how these ideals are perpetuated. You've already thought about mass media in your world, and how the news is spread and communicated. What kind of beauty standards are seen in these places, or encapsulated in the arts?

Perhaps your characters are bombarded with advertisements depicting perfect bodies. Perhaps they exist in a world of augmented reality, where they can live as whatever digital physique they choose to create. Maybe ideal's of beauty are passed down through the generations, with boys encouraged to marry girls with longer necks, or wider hips. Maybe girls without such a body will do whatever they can to achieve it. Even if it harms them. Perhaps boys must win in hand-to-hand combat in order to marry well, training for the battle from the moment they can walk.

And what happens to those who fall short of the standards? Perhaps they struggle to marry, and struggle to marry well. Or maybe they are the ones that are free to marry for love. Perhaps they are shunned, or hidden away, or given the lowliest jobs and positions in society. Maybe they're even barred from marriage, or subjected to forced sterilisation in order to stop their 'defective' genetics from being passed on to a new generation.

Perhaps those who don't match the beauty ideals are the lucky ones. Maybe those who are considered 'perfect' are auctioned off, sacrificed to the Gods, or enslaved as surrogates.

PHYSICAL HEALTH STANDARDS:

MENTAL HEALTH STANDARDS:
WAYS IN WHICH PEOPLE IMPROVE THEIR HEALTH:
HOW SICKNESS AND DISABILITY ARE VIEWED:
THE IDEAL BODY:
HOW BEAUTY IDEALS ARE PERPETUATED:
WHAT HAPPENS TO THOSE WHO FALL SHORT?

UNIVERSAL FEARS

It is generally accepted that we are born with just two innate fears: the fear of loud noises, and the fear of falling. Any others, we pick up along the way. Perhaps through personal experience, such as being bitten by a dog, or as learned behaviour, such as watching someone scream because of a spider.

We all have things we are scared of, but there are also more widespread, universal fears. Fears that are ingrained in a population. Fears that make up part of their culture. These fears are picked up in the same way: through experience and influence.

In a community that suffered a devastating landslide, killing a large percentage of the population, there may be a culturally ingrained fear of heavy rain, or of living near the mountains. Perhaps they hang up talismans in bad weather, or whisper chants and prayers when they pass under the shadow of a mountain. Maybe it's bad luck to curse dry or hot weather, even when the crops are dying. Maybe no one wears blue, or decorates with images of clouds. It might be illegal to fell trees without permission, or to reroute streams or, even, to install a water feature in a garden.

Even generations later, those who didn't directly experience the landslide will pick up these fears through influence. They see the fear in their parents, their grandparents, and learn by example. As all children do.

Eventually, the reason for such fears and superstitions might even be forgotten. Perhaps it becomes a legend about mountain giants, or becomes a myth about a hero that upset a jealous God. Maybe the stories become a way of controlling the people. Maybe the mountains are told to be the resting places of the ancient kings. Kings that guard monsters. Perhaps, should the royal line be disrupted or disputed, the kings will unleash the monsters to restore the bloodline.

These fears can hold fast in a culture for generations. Centuries. Repeated over and over, long after they cease to hold any real value.

It might be a fear of a certain race or species, due to a war centuries before. It might be the tail-end of war propaganda, making out a certain group of people to be savages or barbarians.

Twelve Centuries after the Vikings invaded what is now Britain, us modern Brits still think of them as barbarians who wore horned helmets while they raped and pillaged. While invasions and conquerings are bloody and violent, much of our image of the Vikings is vastly over-exaggerated. In many cases, it's just plain wrong. But ask a British child to draw a Viking, and that horned helmet will be the first thing they draw. Twelve Centuries later, that fearful image persists. Ingrained into our culture.

But it isn't just the past that creates universal fears. The future can do it too. As our world saw the rise of artificial intelligence, we began writing stories about robot uprisings. About humans' enslavement to the machines they, themselves, created. It has become a persistent and repeating theme in popular culture. But it's also not a new idea, this theme of our own creations turning on us. Mary Shelley wrote about it in the early 1800s, in a story that still holds sway.

Zombies are another theme that return over and over. From their origins in witchcraft and black magic, to the modern iteration; mutations caused by released pathogens, or the unexpected side effect of a vaccine.

In simplistic terms, humans like to think of themselves as being at the top of the food chain. Of being the strongest, fastest, and most formidable of creatures. The truth is that we're not. And when we come across something deadly, we fear it. Of course. That's our survival instinct kicking in. But we also like to turn it into stories and examine it. We like to create inventive ways of killing it. And we love stories of the ordinary person, the underdog, becoming the hero and slaying the beast. Because we want to believe that we can do it too.

Universal fears don't always look like monsters, and the reaction to them doesn't always look like fear. Sometimes it looks like humour, as people attempt to lessen the monstrous nature of what they fear. As they attempt to ridicule and belittle it. Sometimes it looks like anger, like prejudice, like hatred. They might dress it up as 'protecting their culture', their 'way of life'. It might manifest as a refusal to change, as a desperate clinging to tradition.

From the burning of heretics to the mistrust of new technology, humans fear the unknown and unfamiliar. Something people don't understand, don't recognise, might just be dangerous. An unfamiliar berry might be poisonous. An identified snake might be venomous. A pair of glowing eyes in the darkness could be just about anything. It keeps us safe, and keeps us alive. Even when it doesn't seem to make sense.

Consider what has happened in the past to instil a particular fear into your population. Consider how this fear is perpetuated in the younger generations. Consider *why* this fear becomes so widespread. Why it matters to their culture.

It may have started out as a way to keep people safe from danger. It may have been vital to their survival. It may, now, be nothing more than cultural stubbornness.

Maybe the younger generation are starting to shrug it off as 'old wives' tales'. Perhaps they start to wear blue and embellish jewellery with clouds and raindrops. Perhaps they fell trees on the mountainside, reroute waterways, and forget to utter their incantations. Maybe they reject the monarchy and demand a democratically elected chamber to rule instead.

Perhaps, after all, the stories were true. Perhaps the monsters are just about to awaken.

UNIVERSAL FEAR:
HISTORICAL REASONING:
HOW THE FEAR MANIFESTS:

UNIVERSAL FEAR:
HISTORICAL REASONING:
HOW THE FEAR MANIFESTS:

UNIVERSAL FEAR:
HISTORICAL REASONING:
HOW THE FEAR MANIFESTS:

A WORD ON INFO DUMPING AND LEARNING CURVES

Once you have completed your worldbuilding, and you are ready to start writing your story, you need to consider how, and how much, of this information to include.

Don't think that you will be including every ounce of what you've worked on. You won't. You shouldn't. I know, I know, you worked hard on it, but it wasn't wasted, even if it never makes it into your book. It helped you to understand your world, so that you can write about it in an informed, attached, and immersive way. So that you can make it all the more real for your readers.

An 'info dump' is the term used for when a writer pours out information onto the page as if they are writing a history text book. It's dry, it's dull and, more often than not, it's confusing.

I'm sure you will have heard the old adage 'show don't tell'. This means that you should be *showing* your readers your worldbuilding, through action and dialogue, not simply *telling* them via a historical lecture.

The absolute best way to teach your readers about your world, is through action. This might be your character clashing with police, or it may simply be them navigating the world.

Let me expand on that: if something in your world is absolutely normal, however far removed it is from our world, if you character treats it, and reacts to it, as if it is entirely regular and everyday, then you are teaching your readers about your world through action.

Say, for example, centaurs are a common sight in your world. If your character treats them with no surprise at all, talking to them as if they are another human, then your readers learn that centaurs and humans live alongside one another equally. Or perhaps your character ridicules, or bullies the centaurs. Or they treat them with respect, or fear. This is what you are teaching your readers about what is the norm in your world. Through action. This is the ideal way to show your worldbuilding.

It's not always so easy.

And so, the next best way is through dialogue. Again, avoid huge blocks of information. This is no different to info dumping, you're simply letting the history lecture come out of a character's mouth. However, they can have a conversation with a friend about a historical aspect of the world, or a cultural aspect. A conversation. Not a lecture.

Sometimes, however, you need to break the rules.

I'm not saying that you must never simply tell your readers information. Sometimes it's necessary. Sometimes it's even the better option. But do it with careful consideration, and do it sparingly. Rules are, certainly in creative pursuits, meant to be broken.

If you're concerned about whether or not you're getting the balance right, the best way is through the use of beta readers. Beta readers read through early, pre-publication versions of books, and give honest feedback that allows the author to improve their story. If you've got the balance wrong, beta readers can tell you.

Another way to learn this is through reading, reading, and reading. Take careful note of how other authors handle the dilemma. How they get the balance right, and how they get it wrong.

The other way is simply through practice. The more you write, the more you drill down into your personal style and voice, the better you are likely to get at it.

The way in which you give worldbuilding information to your readers also depends on the complexity of your world, and how different it is to ours.

If you're writing about earth, whether in the present, past, or future, there are many things your readers will already know. They understand about time, and seasons. They know the animals, the plants. They know what humans are like, and how they interact. The learning curve of your world may be quite a gentle one.

Everything in your world that is different to our real world, adds to the learning curve of your book. Every mythical creature, every imagined technology, every drop of magic, and every jargon word makes that curve a little bit steeper.

You want to ease your readers in. If, in chapter one, you expect them to learn everything about your world and its history, learn who the characters are, and absorb their struggles and goals, they will be exhausted by the time they get to chapter two.

Tell them what they need to know. They don't need 5 million years worth of military history. They may need flashes of it, but not the entire thing. Be gentle with them. Don't make them do too much work, and don't leave them floundering around your story loaded down with too much knowledge.

Again, these are things that you can learn and improve on with the help of beta readers, by reading, reading, reading, and by simply practising your craft. You will find your way, I promise, but I can't tell you how to do it, because we are all different. And our stories are different. And our voices are different.

You might write short 50,000 word novels, and leave a lot of the deeper worldbuilding out. You might write 150,000 word epics, with readers who expect a much more immersive experience. Practice, experiment, and you'll find the right balance for you, your books, and your readers.

IDEAS DUMP

As you work your way through this book, you are bound to have flashes of ideas popping into your mind. Character and story ideas that don't quite belong with the workbook prompts.

Don't lose them; those little flashes are important.

Instead, use the following pages as something of an ideas dump. Some of these may never make it into your finished book, but you never know, you may be able to recycle them into other stories.

No idea is ever wasted...

WANT EVEN MORE WORLDBUILDING?

Our adventures don't have to end here...

You can explore the rest of my series of worldbuilding guides for authors, guiding you through the basics of worldbuilding, helping you to create magic systems and religions, to write dystopian and post-apocalyptic fiction, and to create histories rich with myths and monsters.

Find more information on all of my workbooks and other worldbuilding services at stepbystepworldbuilding.com

Get Your Free Creating a Timeline Worksheet

Join my worldbuilding mailing list to claim your free Creating a Timeline worksheet.

You will also receive all the latest news on releases and workshops, as well as worldbuilding tips, tricks, and resources.

Join at subscribepage.com/worldbuilding

ABOUT ANGELINE TREVENA

Angeline Trevena was born and bred in a rural corner of Devon, but now lives among the breweries and canals of central England with her husband, their two sons, and a rather neurotic cat. She is a dystopian urban fantasy and post-apocalyptic author, a podcaster, and events manager.

In 2003 she graduated from Edge Hill University, Lancashire, with a BA Hons Degree in Drama and Writing. During this time she decided that her future lay in writing words rather than performing them.

Some years ago she worked at an antique auction house and religiously checked every wardrobe that came in to see if Narnia was in the back of it. She's still not given up looking for it.

Find out more at angelinetrevena.co.uk and stepbystepworldbuilding.com

Made in United States
North Haven, CT
06 May 2023